Encyclopedia OF AMAZING FACTS

First published in 2022 by Miles Kelly Publishing Ltd
Harding's Barn, Bardfield End Green, Thaxted, Essex, CM6 3PX, UK

Copyright © Miles Kelly Publishing Ltd 2022

2 4 6 8 10 9 7 5 3 1

Publishing Director Belinda Gallagher
Creative Director Jo Cowan
Editorial Director Rosie Neave
Design Manager Simon Lee
Image Manager Liberty Newton
Production Elizabeth Collins
Reprographics Stephan Davis
Assets Venita Kidwai

All rights reserved. No part of this publication may be reproduced, stored in a retrieval system, or transmitted by any means, electronic, mechanical, photocopying, recording or otherwise, without the prior permission of the copyright holder.

ISBN 978-1-960009-24-1

Printed in China

Made with paper from a sustainable forest

littlehippobooks.com

Encyclopedia OF AMAZING FACTS

Little Hippo Books

CONTENTS

INCREDIBLE SPACE 8–27

Our life-giving star......... 8
The planet family.......... 10
Earth in space............ 12
The Moon................ 14
Earth's neighbors 16
Tiny planets.............. 18
Massive planets 20
Far, far away............. 22
Launching into space...... 24
At home in space 26

ACTIVE EARTH 28–51

Inside Earth.............. 28
Making mountains 30
Lakes and rivers.......... 32
Rivers of ice............. 34
Caves and chambers...... 36
Dry deserts 38
Forests of the world 40
Oceans of the world...... 42
The atmosphere......... 44
What is weather?........ 46
All the seasons.......... 48
The water cycle 50

SUPER SCIENCE   52–67

Our world of science 52
Hot science 54
Light at work 56
What a noise! 58
Magnet power 60
What is electricity? 62
Mighty materials 64
Mini science 66

DEADLY DINOSAURS   68–81

What are dinosaurs? 68
The Age of Dinosaurs 70
Gentle giants 72
Huge hunters 74
Eggs and nests 76
Caring parents 78
Where did they go? 80

FANTASTIC MAMMALS 82–101

What are mammals? 82
Mammal families 84
Big and small 86
Plant food 88
Hungry hunters 90
River mammals 92
Snow mammals 94
Fins and flippers 96
In the rain forest 98
Desert life 100

BRILLIANT BIRDS 102–117

What is a bird? 102
Starting life 104
Bird homes 106
Fast fliers 108
Swimmers and divers 110
Night birds 112
Feeding time 114
Fierce hunters 116

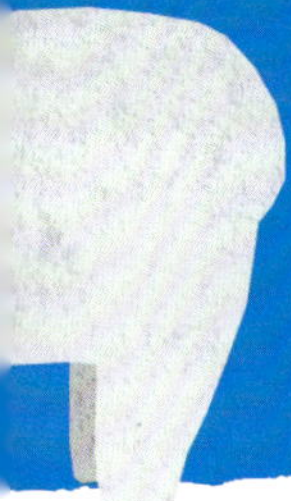

AWESOME BUGS   118–131

What is a bug? 118
The insect world. 120
Taking flight 122
Attack and defend. 124
Hide and seek 126
Dinner time 128
What is a spider? 130

ANCIENT HISTORY   132–155

Life on the Nile. 132
Powerful pharaohs 134
Gods and goddesses 136
The pyramids of Giza 138
Valley of the Kings 140
Preserving the dead 142
The Roman empire. 144
Family life 146
A trip to the baths 148
Roman style 150
The mighty Colosseum 152
In the army 154

Index. 156
Acknowledgments 160

INCREDIBLE SPACE

Our life-giving star

The Sun is our nearest star. To us, it does not look like other stars because it is much closer to Earth. The Sun is not solid like Earth— it is a giant ball of super-hot gases.

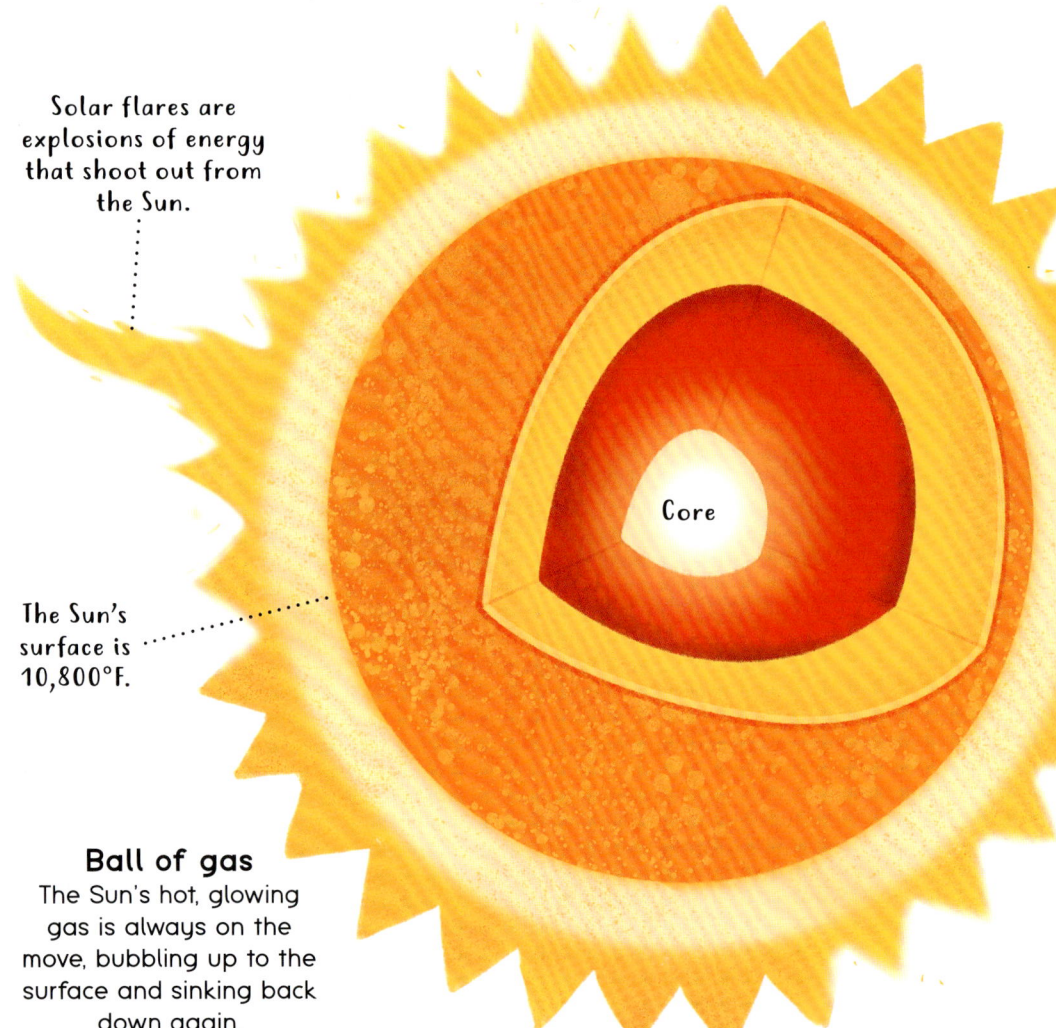

Solar flares are explosions of energy that shoot out from the Sun.

Core

The Sun's surface is 10,800°F.

Ball of gas
The Sun's hot, glowing gas is always on the move, bubbling up to the surface and sinking back down again.

INCREDIBLE SPACE

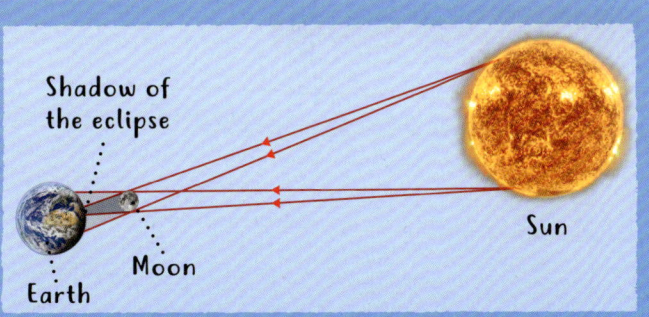

Solar eclipse

Every so often, the Sun, Moon, and Earth line up in space so that the Moon is directly between Earth and the Sun. This stops sunlight from reaching a small area on Earth. The area grows dark and cold, as if nighttime has come early. This is called an eclipse.

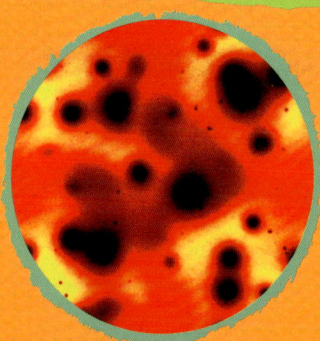

Sunspots may be 2,700°F cooler than other areas on the Sun.

Solar prominences can be huge, with some reaching up to 62,000 miles into space.

Blackout

When the Moon completely covers the Sun, it is called a total eclipse. All that can be seen is the Sun's corona, a ring of white glowing gas. Although the Moon and the Sun look the same size in an eclipse, the Sun is actually 400 times bigger than the Moon, and 400 times further away.

FUN FACT!

The Sun's surface is nearly 60 times hotter than boiling water (212°F). It is so hot, it would melt a spacecraft that flew near it.

INCREDIBLE SPACE

The planet family

The Sun is surrounded by a family of eight circling planets called the Solar System. This family is held together by an invisible force called gravity, which pulls things toward each other. It is the same force that pulls us to the ground and stops us from floating away.

Held in place
The Sun's gravity pulls on the planets and keeps them traveling around it, in circles called orbits. Earth's gravity holds the Moon in its orbit.

Mars

Venus

Earth

Mercury

Jupiter

Sun

INCREDIBLE SPACE

Big and small
The eight planets are all different. Mercury, nearest to the Sun, is small and hot. Venus, Earth, and Mars are rocky and cooler. Beyond them Jupiter, Saturn, Uranus, and Neptune are large and cold.

Neptune

Saturn

Uranus

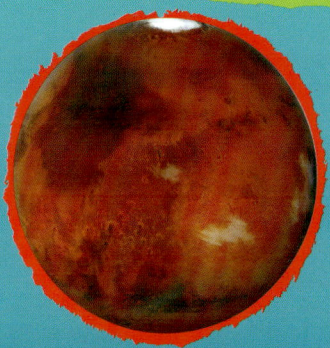

The four planets closest to the Sun are rocky. Mars is covered in **red dust**.

Some planets have rings made of **ice, dust, and rocks**. Saturn is famous for its rings.

Some planets, like Jupiter, have **swirling atmospheres** of gas.

FUN FACT!
If the Sun was the size of a large beach ball, Earth would be as small as a pea, and the Moon would look like a pinhead.

INCREDIBLE SPACE

Earth in Space

Earth moves through space at nearly 10,000 feet per second. It weighs 6,600 million, million, million tons. Up to two-thirds of Earth's rocky surface is covered by water, making the seas and oceans.

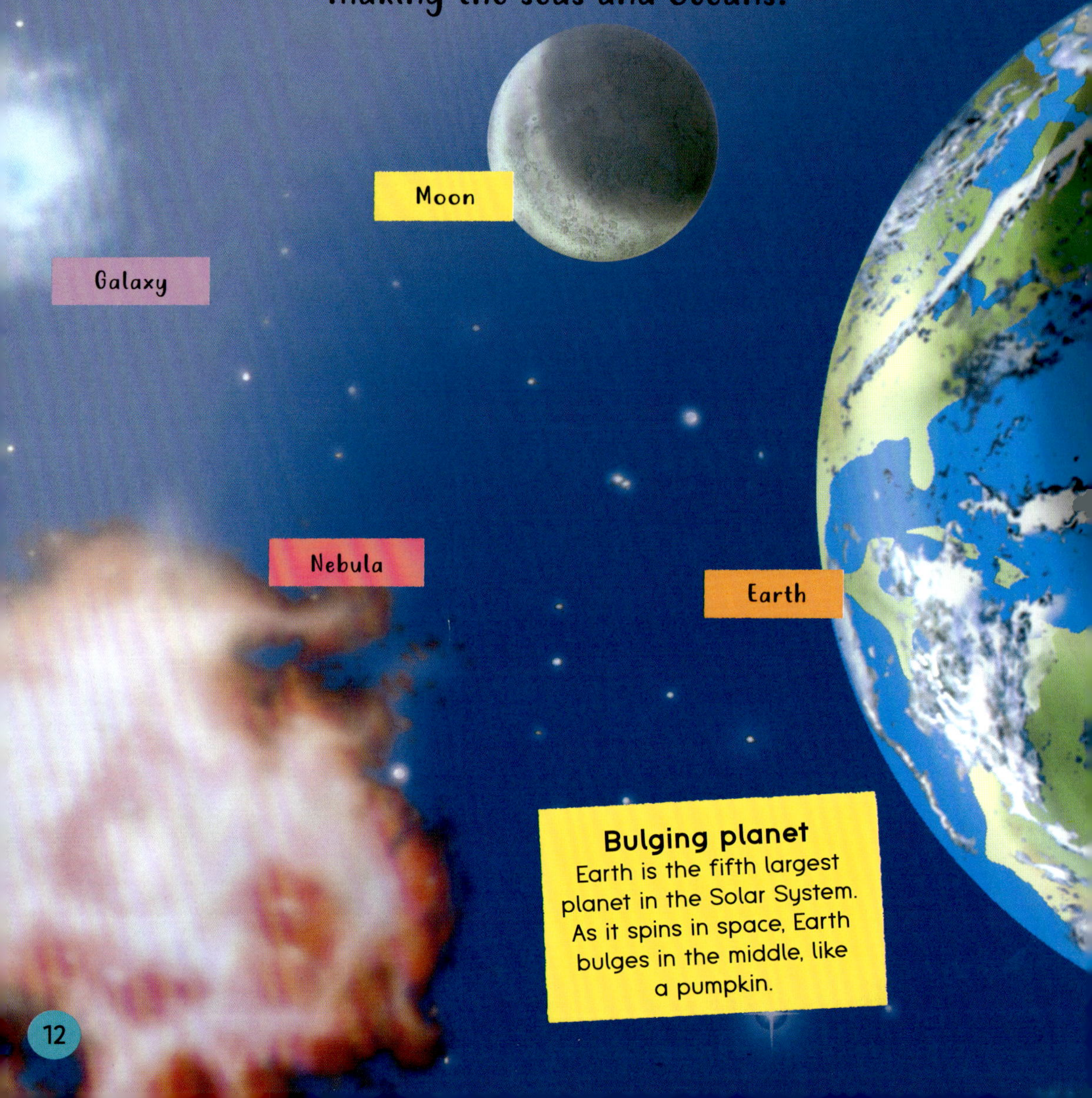

Moon

Galaxy

Nebula

Earth

Bulging planet
Earth is the fifth largest planet in the Solar System. As it spins in space, Earth bulges in the middle, like a pumpkin.

INCREDIBLE SPACE

Our atmosphere
Surrounding Earth is a layer of gases called the atmosphere. It stretches 435 miles from Earth's surface.

Galaxies are giant groups of millions or even trillions of stars.

A cloud of dust and gas in space is called a **nebula**.

A **star** is a ball of very hot gas.

Star

INCREDIBLE SPACE

The Moon

Most planets have moons circling around them. Earth's Moon is one of the largest in the Solar System. Scientists think the Moon was formed over three billion years ago.

Circling Earth
The Moon is very close to Earth. It travels around Earth, taking one month to complete its journey.

Craters are made when rocks crash into the Moon's surface.

Dark areas are low, flat plains called seas.

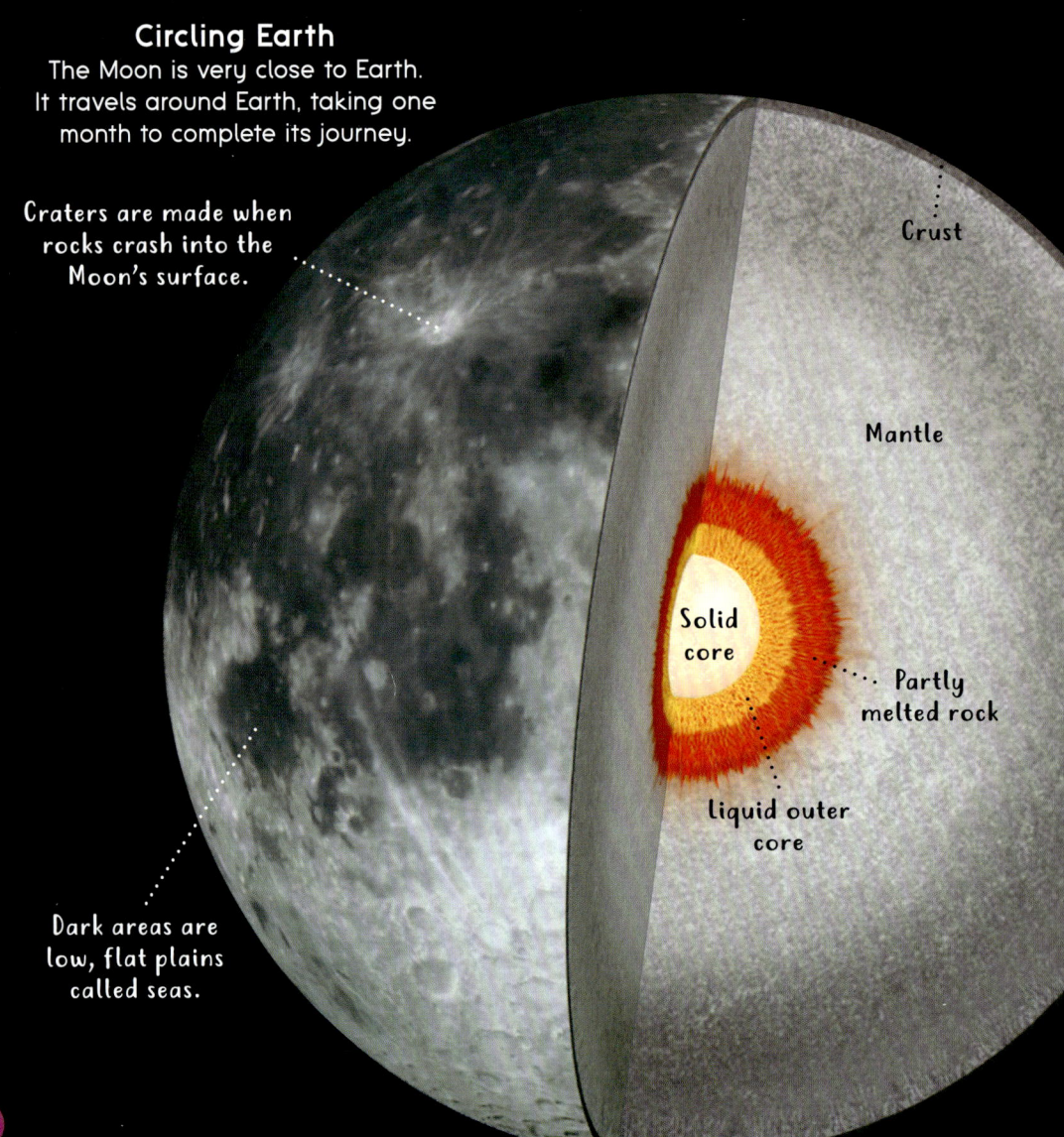

Crust

Mantle

Solid core

Partly melted rock

liquid outer core

INCREDIBLE SPACE

Phases of the Moon

Over one month, the Moon changes from a thin crescent shape to a round shape. This is because as the Sun lights up one side of the Moon, the other side is dark. As the Moon circles the Earth, we see different parts of the lit side.

1. Crescent Moon
2. Half Moon
3. Full Moon
4. Half Moon
5. Crescent Moon

The Moon is a dry, dusty ball of rock. Its surface is covered in hollows called **craters**.

FUN FACT!

There is no air or water on the Moon. When astronauts first went there, they had to take air with them in their spacecraft and spacesuits.

Extra high tides happen when the Sun, Moon, and Earth are aligned.

The Moon's pull of gravity

The Moon and tides

As Earth spins, the Moon's gravity pulls the oceans toward it, creating the tides.

The **far side of the Moon** always faces away from Earth. The near side always faces toward Earth.

INCREDIBLE SPACE

Earth's neighbors

Venus and Mars are the nearest planets to Earth. Venus is closer to the Sun than Earth, and Mars is further away. The time it takes for a planet to circle the Sun is called a year. On Venus a year is 225 days, on Earth 365 days, and on Mars 687 days.

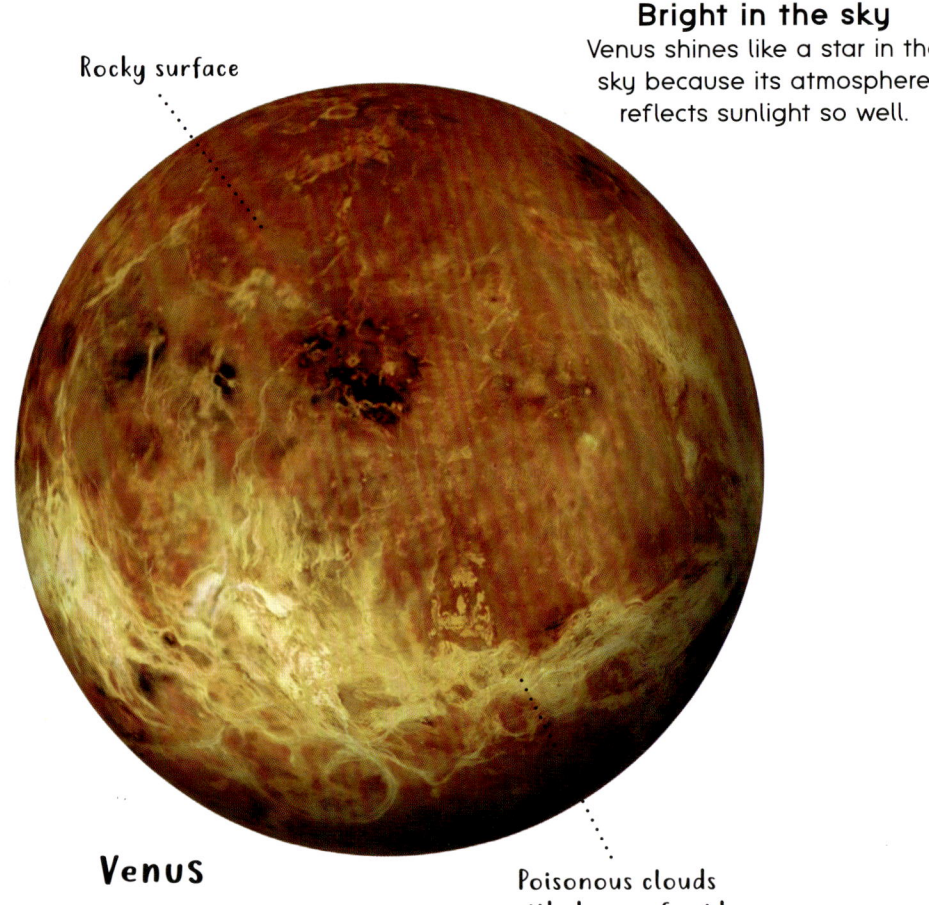

Rocky surface

Bright in the sky
Venus shines like a star in the sky because its atmosphere reflects sunlight so well.

Venus

Poisonous clouds with drops of acid

INCREDIBLE SPACE

Red desert
Mars is very dry, like a desert, and covered in red dust. Winds on Mars whip up huge dust storms that can cover the whole planet.

Olympus Mons is a giant volcano.

Valles Marineris is an enormous valley that cuts across Mars.

Mars

The white ice caps are made of frozen carbon dioxide gas.

Venus has a volcano called **Maat Mons**. It is 3.7 miles high.

Mars has two small moons. **Phobos** is only 17 miles across.

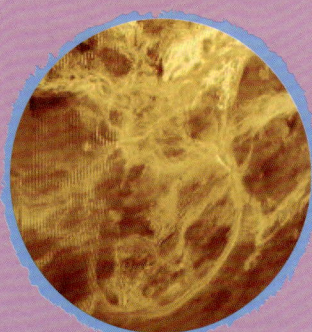

Venus is the **hottest** planet as its clouds trap the Sun's heat.

Planet spotting
See if you can spot Venus in the night sky. It is often the first bright star to appear in the evening, just above where the Sun has set. Sometimes it is called the evening star.

INCREDIBLE SPACE

Tiny planets

Mercury is closest to the Sun. It is a cratered ball of rock and has no atmosphere, so the sunny side is boiling hot, while the other side is freezing cold. Pluto is the biggest dwarf planet. There are five "official" dwarf planets, although many more have been found.

Planet of craters
Mercury has many craters. This shows how often it has been hit by space rocks. One was so large, it shattered rocks on the other side of the planet.

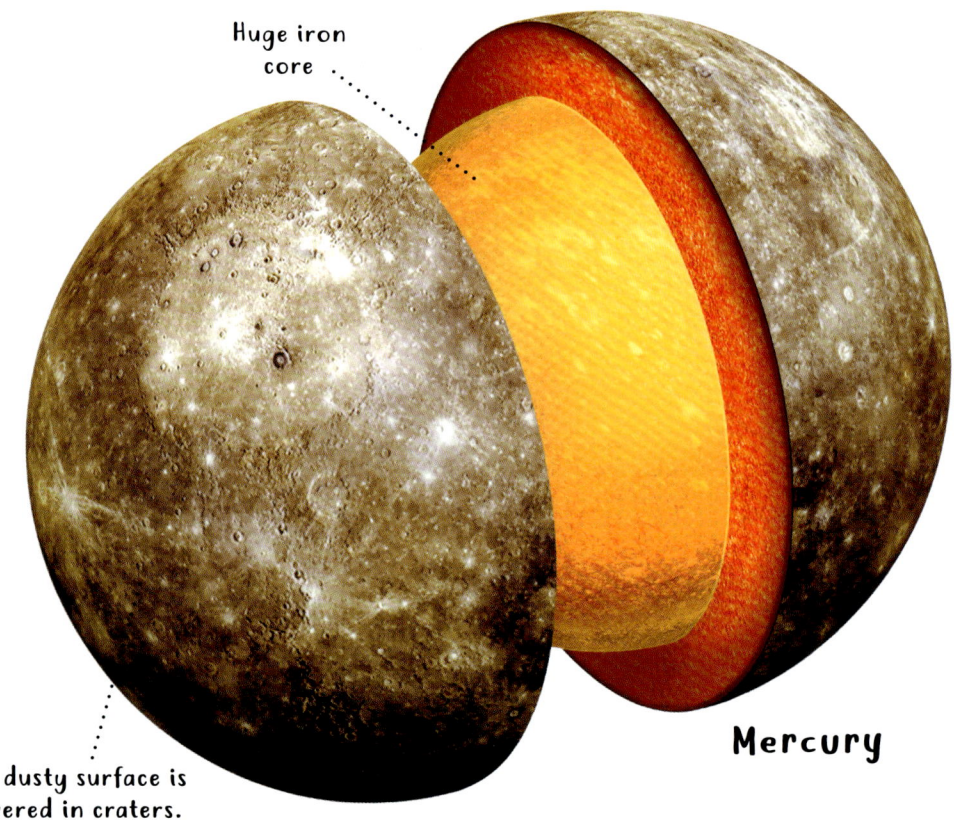

Huge iron core

Mercury

The dusty surface is covered in craters.

INCREDIBLE SPACE

Make craters

You will need
flour • tray • marble or stone

1. Spread some flour about one inch deep in a tray and smooth over the surface.
2. Drop a marble or stone onto the flour and see the saucer-shaped crater that it makes.

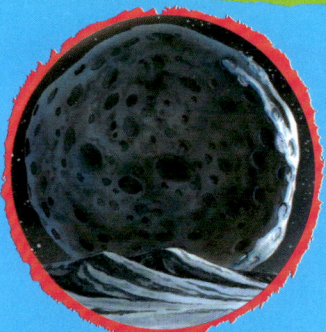

Pluto's moon, **Charon**, was only discovered in 1976.

Change for Pluto

Up until 2006, Pluto was a regular planet. When astronomers started finding other smaller worlds, Pluto was classified as a dwarf planet.

The cratered surface is covered in solid ice.

Sunlit side

Pluto

The Sun looks huge as it rises over Mercury.

FUN FACT!
Eris is the most distant dwarf planet, and is made of rock and ice.

Dwarf planets

Makemake

Ceres

Eris

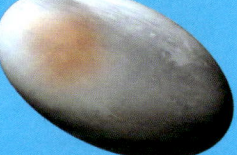
Haumea

Massive planets

Jupiter is the largest planet in the Solar System. It is 11 times wider than Earth, although it is still much smaller than the Sun. Saturn, the next largest planet, is more than nine times as wide as Earth.

Stormy surface
There are many storms on Jupiter, but none as large or as long lasting as the Great Red Spot.

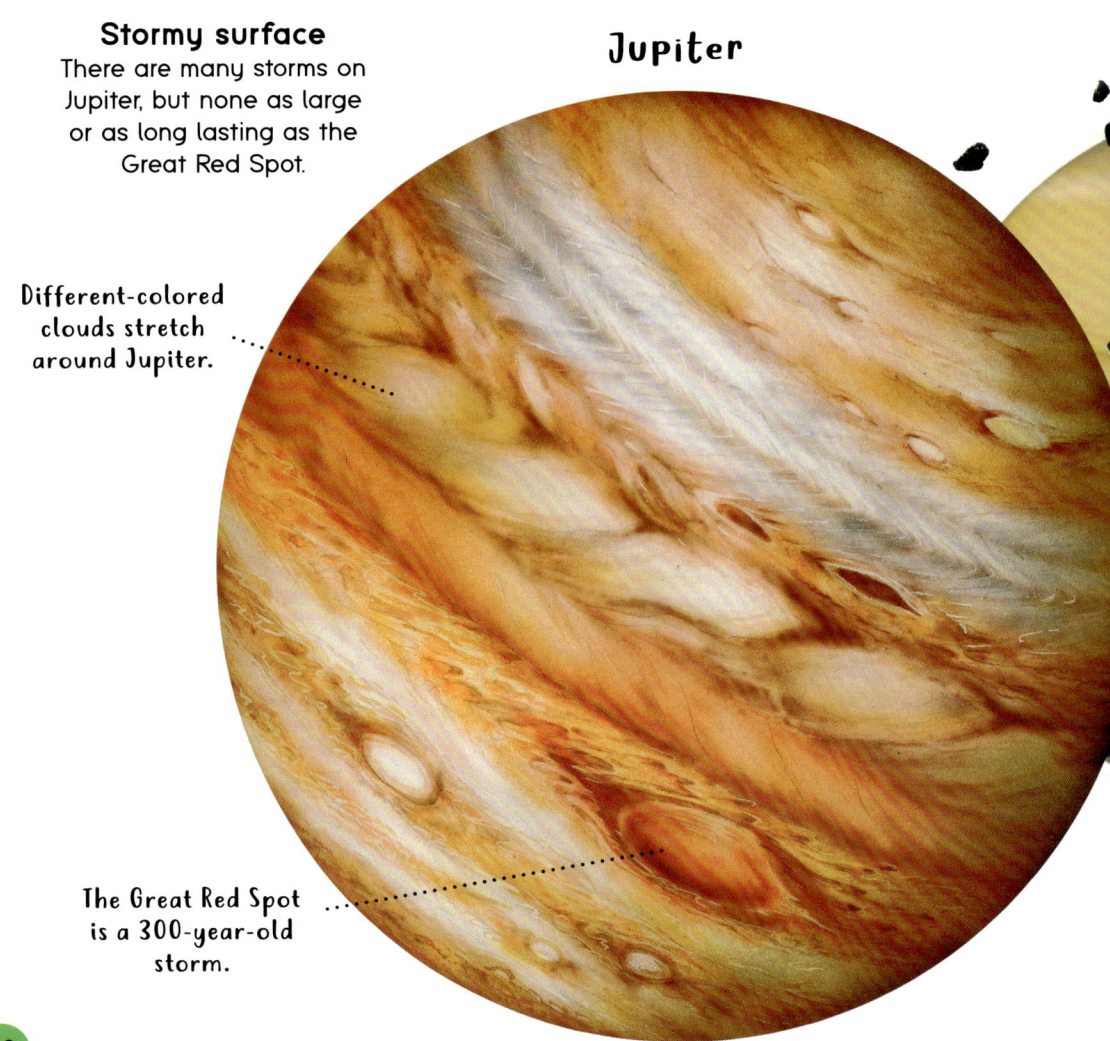

Jupiter

Different-colored clouds stretch around Jupiter.

The Great Red Spot is a 300-year-old storm.

INCREDIBLE SPACE

Saturn's rings
Although Saturn's rings are very wide, they stretch out in a very thin layer around the planet.

The **Galilean moons** are Jupiter's four biggest moons. They were discovered by Italian astronomer Galileo Galilei (1564–1642).

Saturn

Yellow clouds stretch to make faint bands.

Io   Callisto

Europa   Ganymede

Jupiter's biggest moon is Ganymede, and it is also the biggest in the entire Solar System.

Distant giant
From Earth, Saturn looks like a faint but bright yellow star in the sky.

Saturn's shining rings are made of millions of chunks of ice.

FUN FACT!
Saturn is the lightest planet in the Solar System. It would float like a cork in water.

21

INCREDIBLE SPACE

Far, far away

Uranus and Neptune are gas giants like Jupiter and Saturn. They are the next two planets beyond Saturn but much smaller, less than half as wide. Their surfaces are made of liquid and gas.

Uranus

Rings of ice and dust

Sideways spin
Most planets spin upright, but Uranus spins on its side. It may have been knocked over when something crashed into it millions of years ago.

Covered with clouds

Miranda   Ariel   Umbriel

Titania   Oberon

Famous moons
Uranus has 27 moons. Many of them are named after characters from the plays of Shakespeare. Titania is the biggest moon.

INCREDIBLE SPACE

Windy planet
Neptune's winds are the fastest in the Solar System, at 1,500 miles per hour.

Neptune

Storm patches come and go every few years.

Wispy clouds

Uranus has 13 rings. They reflect less light so are harder to see.

Neptune's **dark spot** was a storm, first seen in 1989. It has since gone, but other spots have appeared.

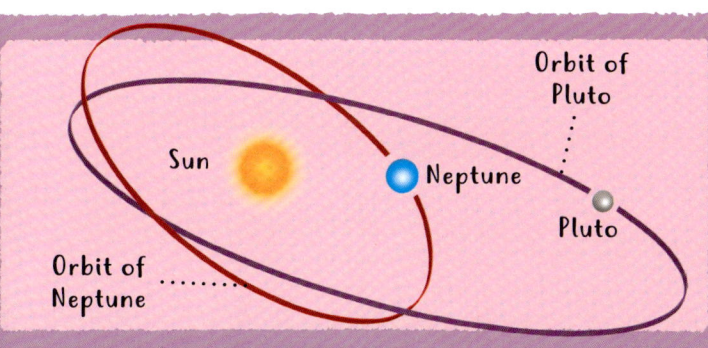

Orbit of Pluto

Sun

Neptune

Pluto

Orbit of Neptune

Long orbits
Neptune is so far from the Sun that its orbit lasts 164.79 Earth years. It has only completed one orbit since it was discovered in 1846. Pluto's orbit is even longer at 248 Earth years.

FUN FACT!
Neptune is the farthest planet from the Sun at 2,800 miles.

INCREDIBLE SPACE

Launching into Space

To blast into space, a rocket has to travel nearly 40 times faster than a jumbo jet. If it goes any slower, gravity pulls it back to Earth. Rockets are powered by burning fuel.

Ariane 5

1. Satellite payload
2. Second stage
3. Liquid oxygen tank
4. First stage
5. Booster rocket
6. Liquid hydrogen fuel tank
7. Solid fuel
8. First stage engine

Blast off!

An Ariane 5 rocket has two stages and two solid rocket boosters to launch satellites into orbit. The boosters burn their fuel in about two minutes, then fall away into the sea.

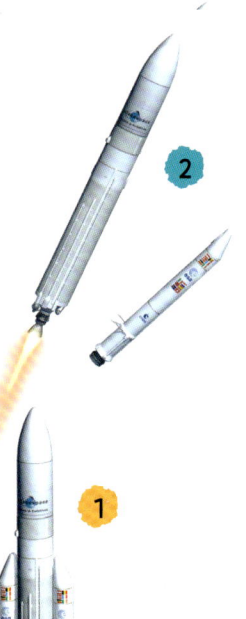

INCREDIBLE SPACE

FUN FACT!
Spacecraft are tested while they are still in orbit around Earth. This is to make sure that all the parts are working properly.

Ariane 5 launch

1. Lift-off
2. Boosters fall away
3. First stage separates
4. Second stage puts satellite into orbit

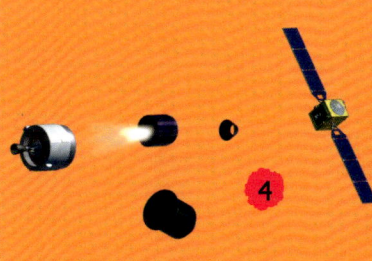

A spacecraft carried by a rocket is called its **payload**.

Make a rocket

You will need
sheet of card (heavy paper) • cardboard tube
sticky tape • scissors

1. Use the tube for the main body of the rocket. Make a cone shape with some of the card and stick it to one end.
2. In a safe place, "launch" the rocket by throwing it up at an angle. It should tumble out of control.
3. Add fins by sticking four large, card triangles to the base. Now it should fly much straighter.

Different-sized rockets are used for different-sized spacecraft.

25

INCREDIBLE SPACE

At home in space

A space station is a home in space for astronauts. It has a kitchen, cabins with sleeping bags, toilets, washbasins, and sometimes showers. There are also places to work and controls where astronauts can check that everything is working properly.

Building the ISS
The International Space Station is the only base in space. It was built in space using different pieces. The first piece was launched in 1998.

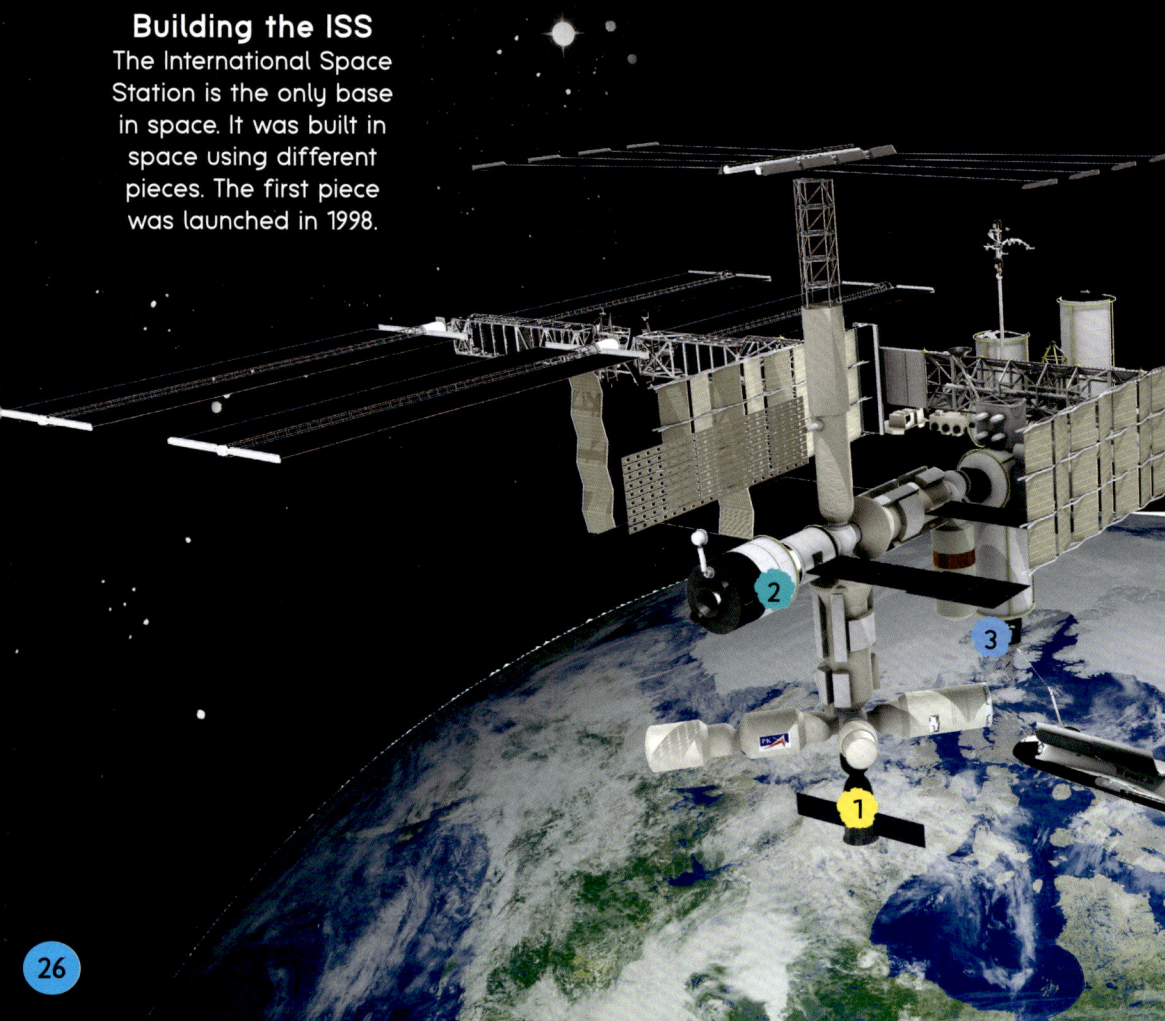

INCREDIBLE SPACE

Key

1. Spacecraft transports astronauts to and from the ISS
2. Astronauts sleep inside the living module
3. Visiting spacecraft join the ISS at docking ports
4. Solar panels always point toward the Sun

FUN FACT!

The US space station Skylab, launched in 1973, fell back to Earth in 1979. Most of it landed in the ocean but some pieces hit Australia.

Living in space

There are six astronauts on board the ISS. They carry out important research about space and test equipment.

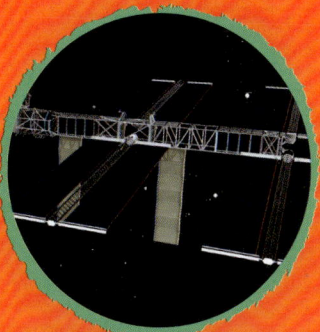

Solar panels use sunlight to make electricity for the ISS.

The ISS can leave a **trail of light** across the sky.

ACTIVE EARTH

Inside Earth

Earth is made up of many different layers. We live on the outer layer—the thin, rocky crust that is covered with land and water.

The layers of Earth
As well as the crust, Earth has a solid mantle and a core. The outer part of the core is liquid, but the inner core is made of solid metal.

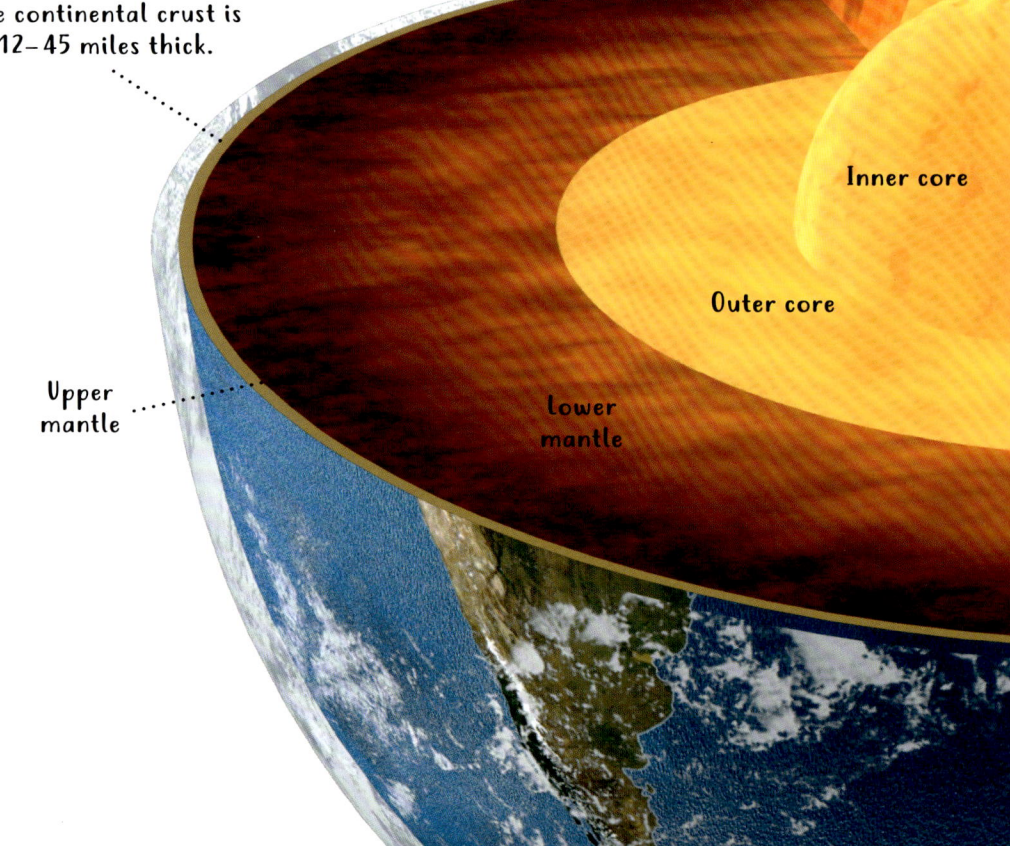

The continental crust is 12–45 miles thick.

Upper mantle

Lower mantle

Outer core

Inner core

ACTIVE EARTH

The crust is divided into chunks of rock called plates.

Atmosphere

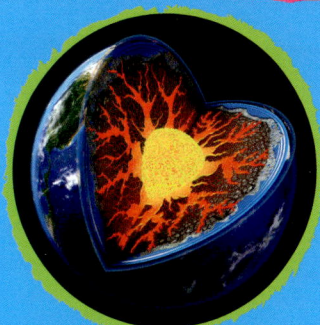

Earth's liquid **inner core** is very hot—10,800°F.

Molten rock can burst through the crust, creating volcanoes.

Oceans and landmasses called **continents** cover Earth's surface.

FUN FACT!
Slow-flowing mantle beneath the Earth's crust means the continents are moving! North America is moving 1.2 inches from Europe every year.

ACTIVE EARTH

Making mountains

It takes millions of years for mountains to form. Young mountains are the highest, but the peaks are made of soft rocks so they break down easily. Underneath are harder rocks that wear away over a longer period of time.

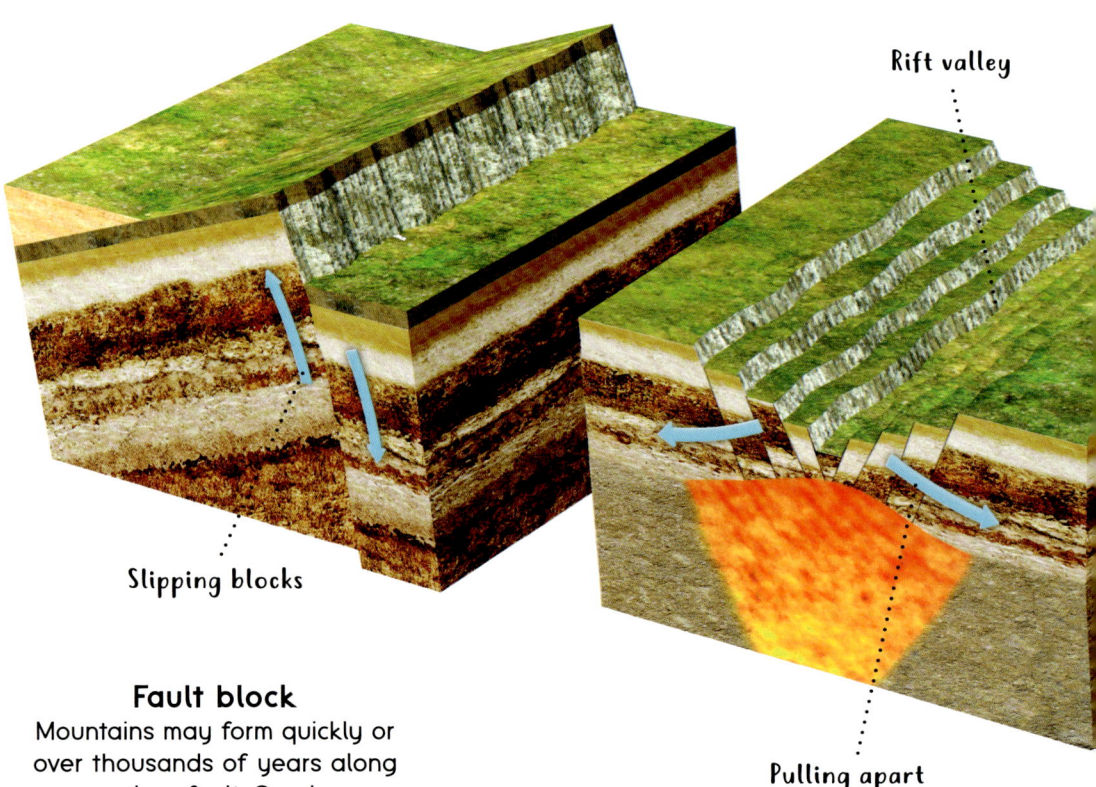

Rift valley

Slipping blocks

Pulling apart

Fault block
Mountains may form quickly or over thousands of years along a crack or fault. One huge block of rock may slip up or down against another.

Rift fault
As rock blocks slide away from each other, there may be volcanic eruptions.

ACTIVE EARTH

Highest peaks
Many mountaintops are so high that they sit above the clouds.

Mountain peaks are often covered in snow.

Subduction
When two plates push together, one may slide below the other, causing the edge to rumple into mountains.

Mountaineers are people who climb mountains.

Sliding below

FUN FACT!
The highest mountain in the world is Mount Everest, which is part of the Himalayas. It is 29,032 feet tall.

ACTIVE EARTH

Lakes and rivers

A mighty river can start from a small spring, where water flows from the ground. The trickle of water from a spring is called a stream. When streams join together, they make a river.

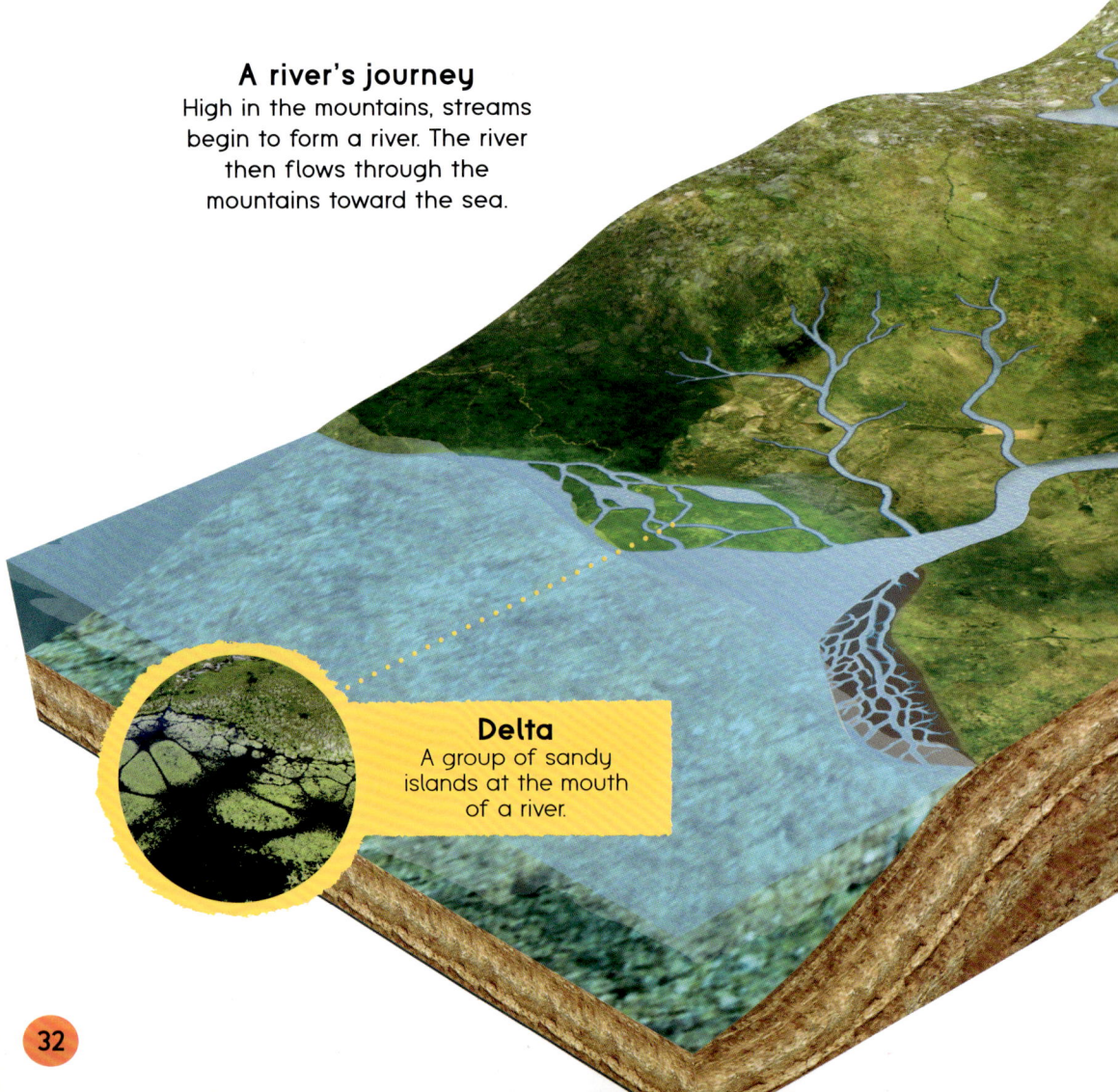

A river's journey
High in the mountains, streams begin to form a river. The river then flows through the mountains toward the sea.

Delta
A group of sandy islands at the mouth of a river.

ACTIVE EARTH

Stream
A small river of water that comes from a spring.

FUN FACT!
Most lakes are blue, but some are green, pink, red, or even white. The colors are made by tiny creatures called algae or by minerals in the water.

A **waterfall** forms when a river flows over a ledge.

Meander
A bend in a river as it winds down to the sea.

A **lake** is a large body of water surrounded by land.

Oxbow lake
A lake that forms when meanders separate from the main river.

ACTIVE EARTH

Rivers of ice

Glaciers are huge areas of ice that form near mountaintops. They slide slowly down the mountainside and melt. As a glacier moves, some rocks break off and are carried along.

Area where the glacier forms.

Melting ice
The end of a glacier is called the "snout." This is where the ice starts to melt, causing large chunks called icebergs to break off into the ocean.

Cracks in the ice are called crevasses.

ACTIVE EARTH

Make an iceberg

You will need
plastic container • clear bowl • water

1. Fill the container with water and put it in the freezer until it is frozen. This is your iceberg.
2. Remove the iceberg from the container. Fill the clear bowl with water and add your iceberg.
3. Look through the side of the bowl to see how much of your iceberg is underwater and what shape it makes.

On the flow
On high mountains, glaciers flow downhill until they reach warmer air and start to melt. At the poles, many glaciers flow straight into the sea.

Snout

Melted ice, called meltwater, can be as small as a puddle or as big as a lake.

U-shaped valleys are made as glaciers push and scrape soil and rock.

Glacial ice melts and crashes into the sea.

Mushroom stones can be formed when glaciers cut away the bottom part of the rock.

ACTIVE EARTH

Caves and chambers

Rocks can be worn away by rainwater trickling into tiny cracks and crevices. Over millions of years, this creates caves, chambers, and waterfalls underground.

Stalactites and stalagmites

Stalagmites grow up from the floor of caves and stalactites grow down from the roof. Over time, they can join together. They are made of the minerals in water.

ACTIVE EARTH

Dissolving rock

Rainwater contains chemicals that can turn it into a weak acid. Acidic rainwater can slowly dissolve rock, especially limestone, when it trickles through any cracks.

FUN FACT!

The largest cave in the world is the Sarawak Chamber in Malaysia. At 2,000 feet long and 1,400 feet wide, you could fit eight Boeing 747 airplanes inside it.

Waterfall in a shaft (vertical cave)

Gallery (horizontal cave)

Stalactites

Stalagmites

Caves have been discovered full of **crystals**. The crystals are made of minerals.

Some spectacular **cave formations** are thousands of years old.

ACTIVE EARTH

Dry deserts

The driest places on Earth are deserts. In many deserts there is a short period of rain every year, but some have dry weather for many years.

Polar deserts

Antarctica is a polar desert. There is hardly any rain and the warmest temperature is less than 50°F.

ACTIVE EARTH

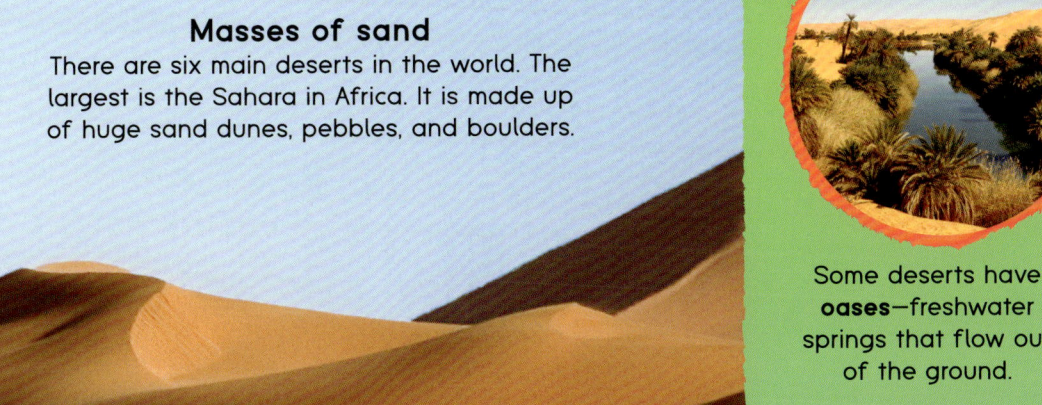

Masses of sand
There are six main deserts in the world. The largest is the Sahara in Africa. It is made up of huge sand dunes, pebbles, and boulders.

Some deserts have **oases**—freshwater springs that flow out of the ground.

Camels have broad feet that stop them from sinking in the sand.

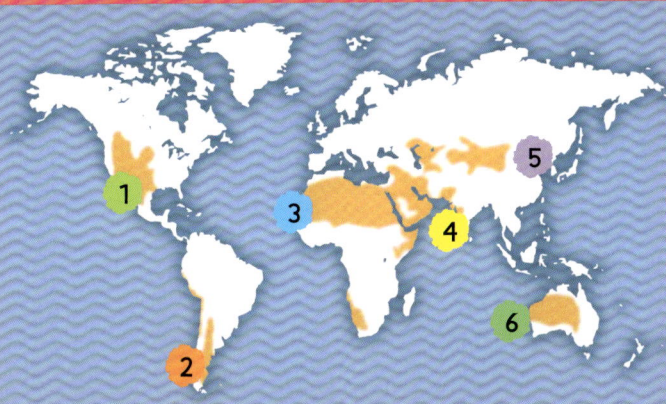

Deserts around the world

1. Great Basin and Mojave
2. Atacama
3. Sahara
4. Arabian
5. Gobi
6. Great Sandy, Gibson, Great Victoria, Simpson

Desert roses are formed when sand joins with minerals.

39

ACTIVE EARTH

Forests of the world

There are three main types of forest—coniferous, temperate, and rain forest. In coniferous forests, the trees stay in leaf all year round. In temperate woodland, deciduous trees lose their leaves in winter.

Wet forests
In rain forests, large numbers of trees and plants grow close together. It rains almost every day. The vegetation is so thick, it can take a raindrop ten minutes to fall to the ground.

Forests types around the world

1. Coniferous forest
2. Temperate forest
3. Tropical forest

ACTIVE EARTH

Toucan

Perfect habitat
Trees provide homes, or habitats, for millions of animals and plants.

The **Amazon rain forest** is the largest tropical rain forest in the world.

Squirrels live in both temperate and coniferous forests.

Fall leaves
In deciduous forests, the leaves turn orange, yellow, and brown as they start to drop in fall. New leaves grow in spring.

The **redwood** is the tallest tree in the world—more than 330 feet in height.

ACTIVE EARTH

Oceans of the world

More than two-thirds of Earth's rocky surface is covered by oceans. Their total area is about 140 million square miles, which means there is more than twice as much ocean as land!

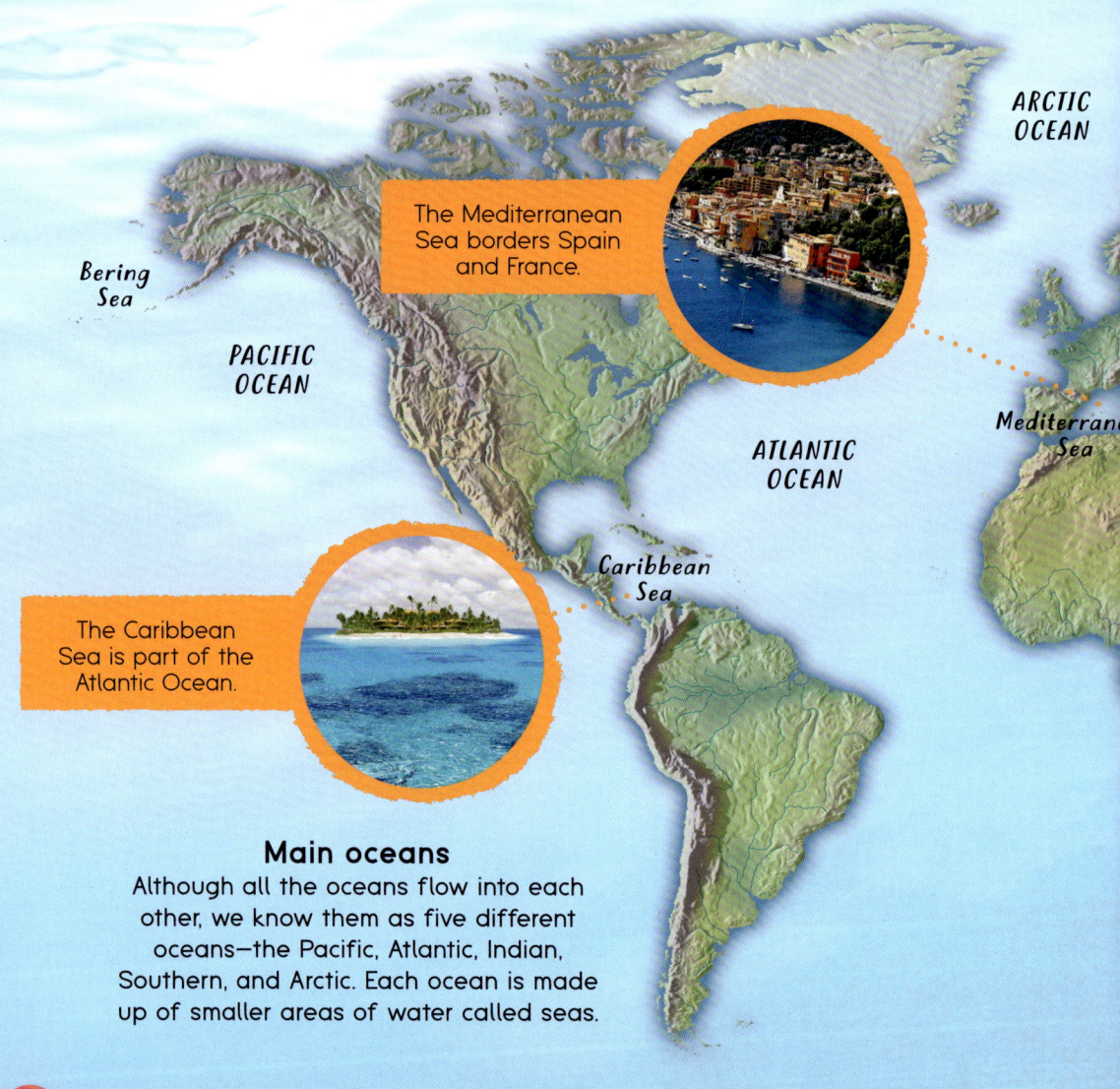

The Mediterranean Sea borders Spain and France.

The Caribbean Sea is part of the Atlantic Ocean.

Main oceans
Although all the oceans flow into each other, we know them as five different oceans—the Pacific, Atlantic, Indian, Southern, and Arctic. Each ocean is made up of smaller areas of water called seas.

ACTIVE EARTH

FUN FACT!
The average depth of the Pacific is more than 13,000 feet, making it the world's deepest ocean.

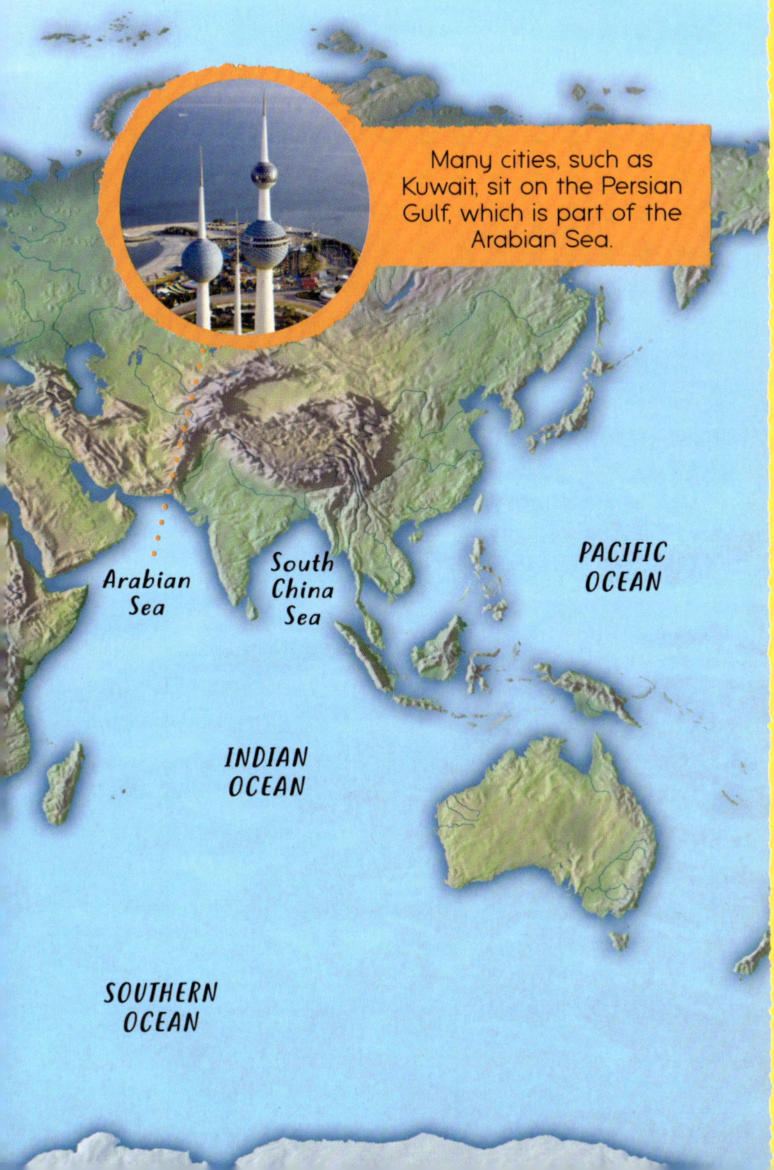

Many cities, such as Kuwait, sit on the Persian Gulf, which is part of the Arabian Sea.

Arabian Sea

South China Sea

PACIFIC OCEAN

INDIAN OCEAN

SOUTHERN OCEAN

Hydrothermal vents are underwater chimneys that spurt hot water and minerals.

Ocean waves carve rocks into amazing shapes such as **sea stacks**.

Icebergs break away from huge glaciers and then drift and melt into the ocean.

43

ACTIVE EARTH

The atmosphere

Our planet is wrapped in a blanket of air called the atmosphere. It stretches for hundreds of miles above our heads. Without an atmosphere, there would be no weather.

Earth from above
The atmosphere keeps in heat, especially at night when part of the planet faces away from the Sun. During the day, it becomes a sunscreen instead.

Oxygen to breathe
The higher up you go, the less oxygen there is in the air. We need oxygen to breathe, so mountaineers wear special breathing equipment when climbing high peaks.

ACTIVE EARTH

Layers of air
The atmosphere stretches right into space. Scientists have split it into five layers, or spheres.

Exosphere
120–600 miles

Thermosphere
50–120 miles

Mesosphere
30–50 miles

Stratosphere
6–30 miles

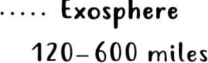

Troposphere
0–6 miles

Low-level satellites orbit within the outer layers of the atmosphere.

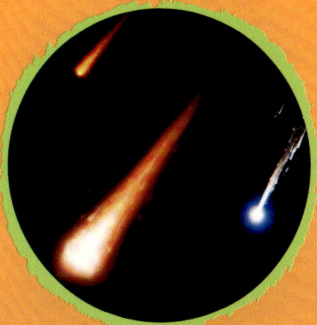

Meteorites are pieces of rock from space that fall through the atmosphere to Earth's surface.

Planes fly just above the clouds, where the air is thinner.

ACTIVE EARTH

What is weather?

Rain, sunshine, and snow are all types of weather. In parts of the world, such as near the Equator, the weather is nearly always the same. Most of the world has a temperate climate, meaning the weather changes daily.

The world's climates
The colored rings show the different climates around the world. In general, the warmest climates are found close to the Equator.

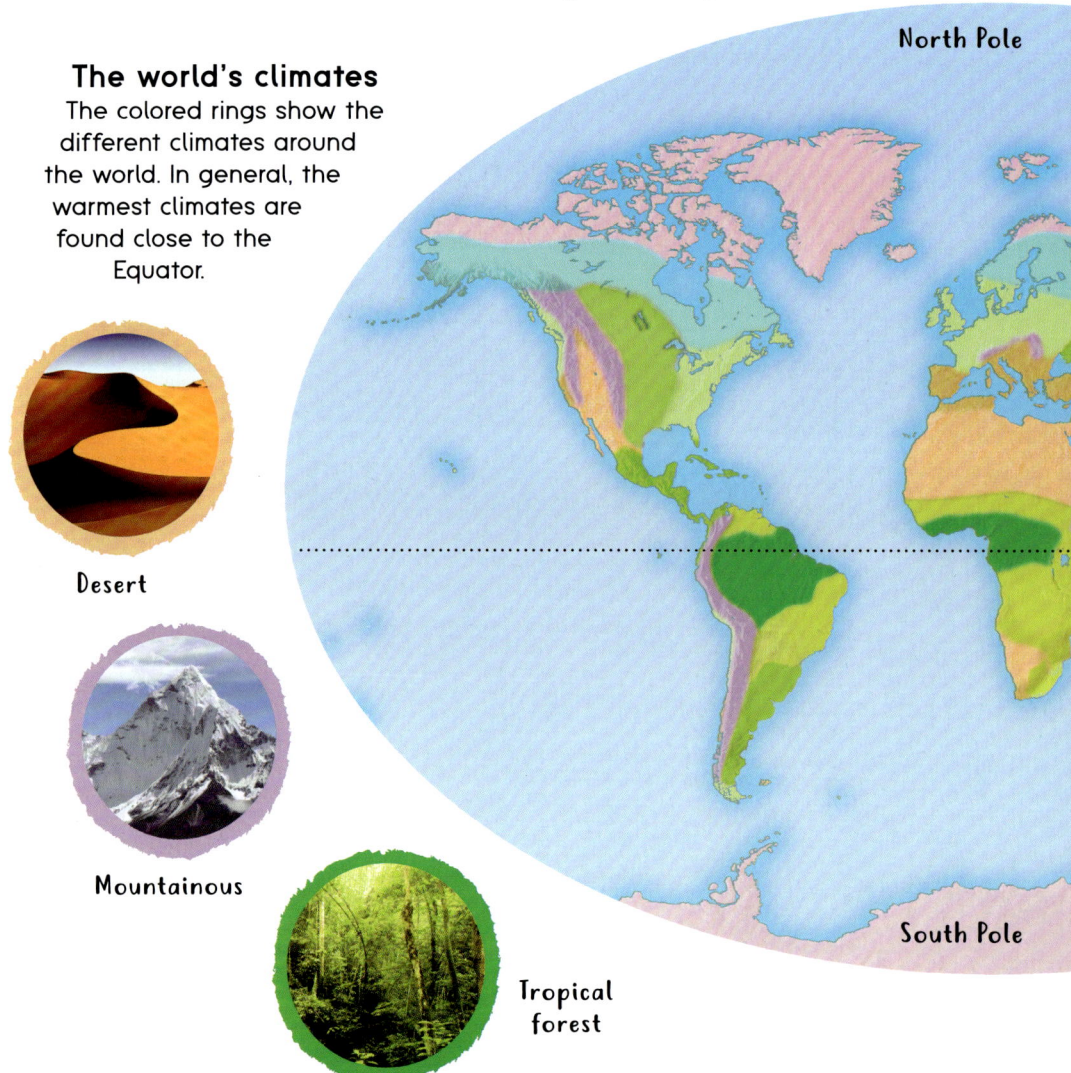

Desert

Mountainous

Tropical forest

North Pole

South Pole

ACTIVE EARTH

Polar climates
The coldest climates in the world are found at the North and South poles. They are furthest from the Equator, and so it is cold and icy all year round.

Tropical grassland

Temperate grassland

Rain forests are very hot but they also have daily downpours of rain.

Polar

Mountains can be very cold and covered in snow.

Equator

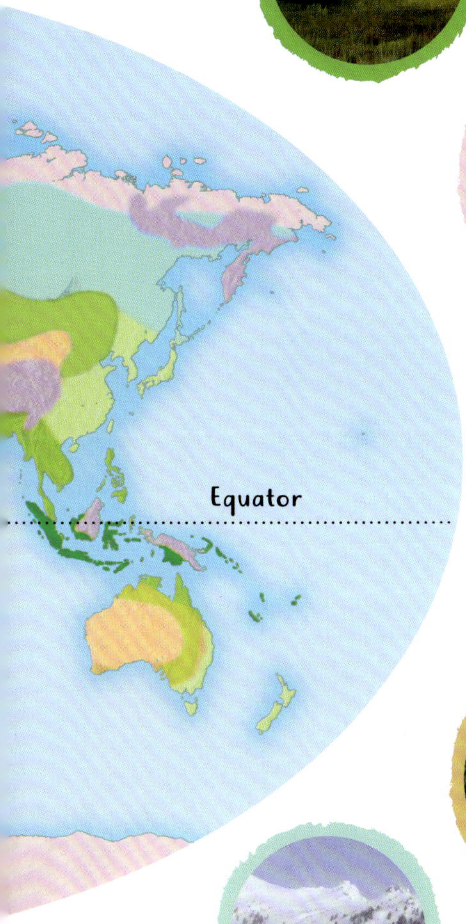

Wet temperate

Dry temperate

Cold temperate

Deserts are home to many plants and animals, such as lizards, that can survive in the heat.

47

ACTIVE EARTH

All the Seasons

The seasons are caused by Earth's movement around the Sun. It takes one year for Earth to orbit the Sun. Earth is tilted, so over the year the North and South poles take turns facing toward the Sun, giving us seasons.

Spring in the Northern Hemisphere (March–May)
The temperature begins to get warmer. Flowers bloom, and trees start to grow their leaves again.

Sun

Summer in the Northern Hemisphere (June–September)
In June, the North Pole leans toward the Sun. The Sun heats the northern half of Earth, making it summertime.

ACTIVE EARTH

Sunshine at midnight
At the North Pole during the height of summer, the Sun never disappears below the horizon.

In **summer**, people like to enjoy the sunshine by going to the beach.

Winter in the Northern Hemisphere
(December–March)
In December, the North Pole leans away from the Sun, meaning it is winter.

FUN FACT!
Seasons in the Southern Hemisphere are the opposite to those in the north. Spring starts in September and summer begins in December. Fall is in March, and Winter begins in June!

In northern **winter**, people ski and snowboard on snowy slopes.

Fall in the Northern Hemisphere
(October–November)
In fall, many forests change color, from green to golden brown. Trees prepare for winter by losing their leaves.

ACTIVE EARTH

The water cycle

The water cycle involves all the water on Earth. Water vapor rises from lakes, rivers, and the sea to form clouds in the atmosphere.

Water, water, everywhere
Too much rain causes flooding. Flash floods happen after a short burst of heavy rainfall.

1 Water evaporates (disappears into the air) from the sea.

5 The rivers run back to the sea, and the cycle starts again.

From sea to sky
As the Sun heats the ocean's surface, some water turns into water vapor (a kind of gas) and rises into the air to form clouds. Rain falls from the clouds, some of which is soaked up by the land, but a lot finds its way back to the sea.

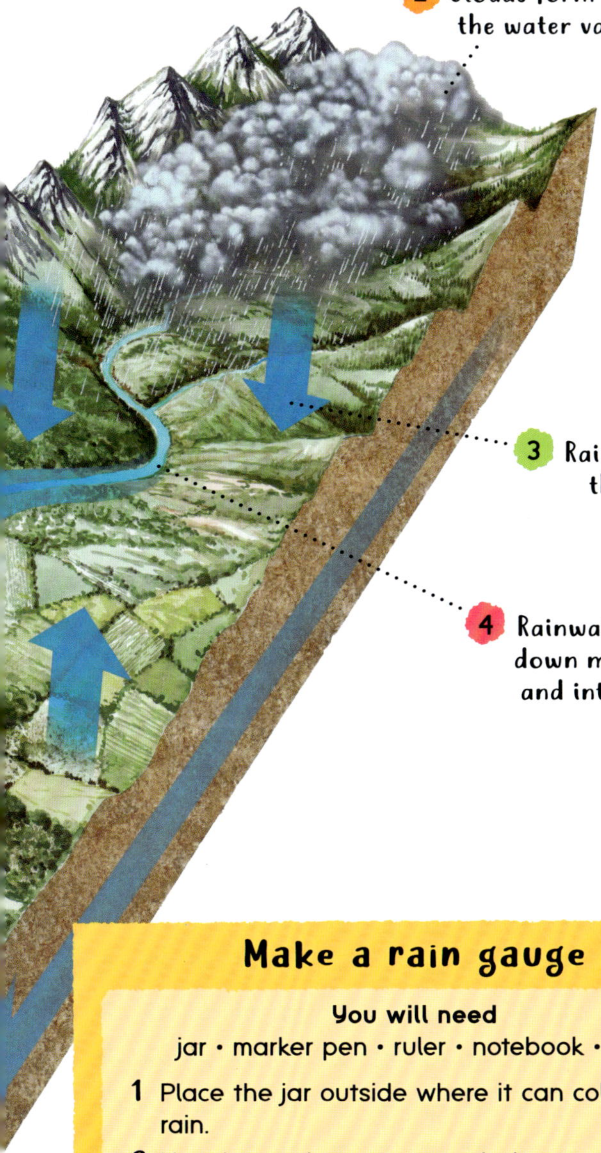

ACTIVE EARTH

2 Clouds form from the water vapor.

3 Rain falls from the clouds.

4 Rainwater flows down mountains and into rivers.

Cumulonimbus clouds give heavy rain showers.

Stratus clouds can bring drizzle or appear as fog.

Cirrus clouds look like wisps of smoke. They are unlikely to bring rain.

Make a rain gauge

You will need
jar • marker pen • ruler • notebook • pen

1 Place the jar outside where it can collect rain.

2 Use the marker pen to mark the water level on the outside of the jar each day.

3 Keep a record of the changing levels of rainfall in a notebook.

SUPER SCIENCE

Our world of science

Science is all around us. Toasters, bicycles, cell phones, cars, computers, light bulbs—all the gadgets and machines we use every day are the result of scientific discoveries.

Feeling forces
Pushes and pulls make things stop and start. Scientists use the word "force" for pushes and pulls. Forces are all around us. The force of gravity pulls things downward. It makes a rollercoaster car hurtle downhill.

SUPER SCIENCE

Hidden strength

Skyscrapers stay up because they have a strong frame on the inside. The frame is made from steel and concrete. These are very strong materials. The frame is hidden by the skyscraper's walls.

Electricity powers machines and gadgets. It can be harnessed from the wind.

We have **transport** like cars, trains, and planes because of scientific discoveries.

Space exploration is a type of science.

SUPER SCIENCE

Hot Science

Heat is vital in many ways. We cook with heat, warm our homes, and heat water. It is also used in factories to make all kinds of things from steel to toys.

Fizz! Crackle! Bang!
Fireworks flash and bang because they are full of chemicals that burn. The chemicals have lots of energy stored in them. When they burn, the energy changes to light, heat, and sound.

How candles burn
When the candle wick is lit, the wax around it melts. The wick soaks up the liquid wax and the heat of the flame turns the wax into a gas (vapor), which burns away. As the wax becomes vapor it cools the wick, allowing the candle to burn slowly.

SUPER SCIENCE

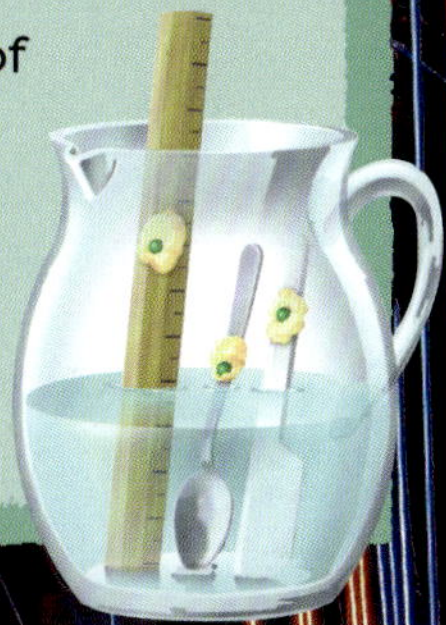

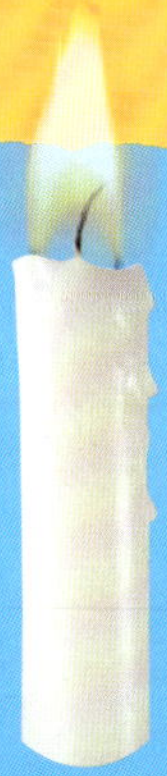

Hot air rises from a candle. This movement of heat is called **convection**.

A hot drink passes its heat to the spoon, warming it up. Heat moves by **conduction**.

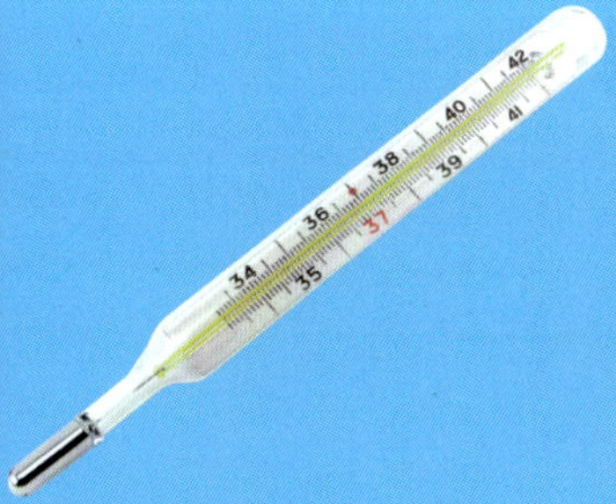

A **thermometer** is used for measuring heat.

Carrying heat

You will need
frozen peas • butter • wooden ruler
metal spoon • plastic spatula • heatproof jug

1. Place a pat of butter on the end of a ruler, spoon, or spatula, and place a pea on each pat of butter to stick.
2. Put the other ends in a heatproof jug. Ask an adult to fill the jug with hot water.
3. Heat is conducted (passed on) from the water, up the object, to melt the butter. Which object is the best conductor?

SUPER SCIENCE

Light at work

Light is energy that you can see. Light waves are tiny. About 2,000 of them laid end to end would stretch across this period.

Splitting light
Light rays travel in straight lines. When sunlight (white light) passes through a prism it splits into a spectrum of colors, like a rainbow.

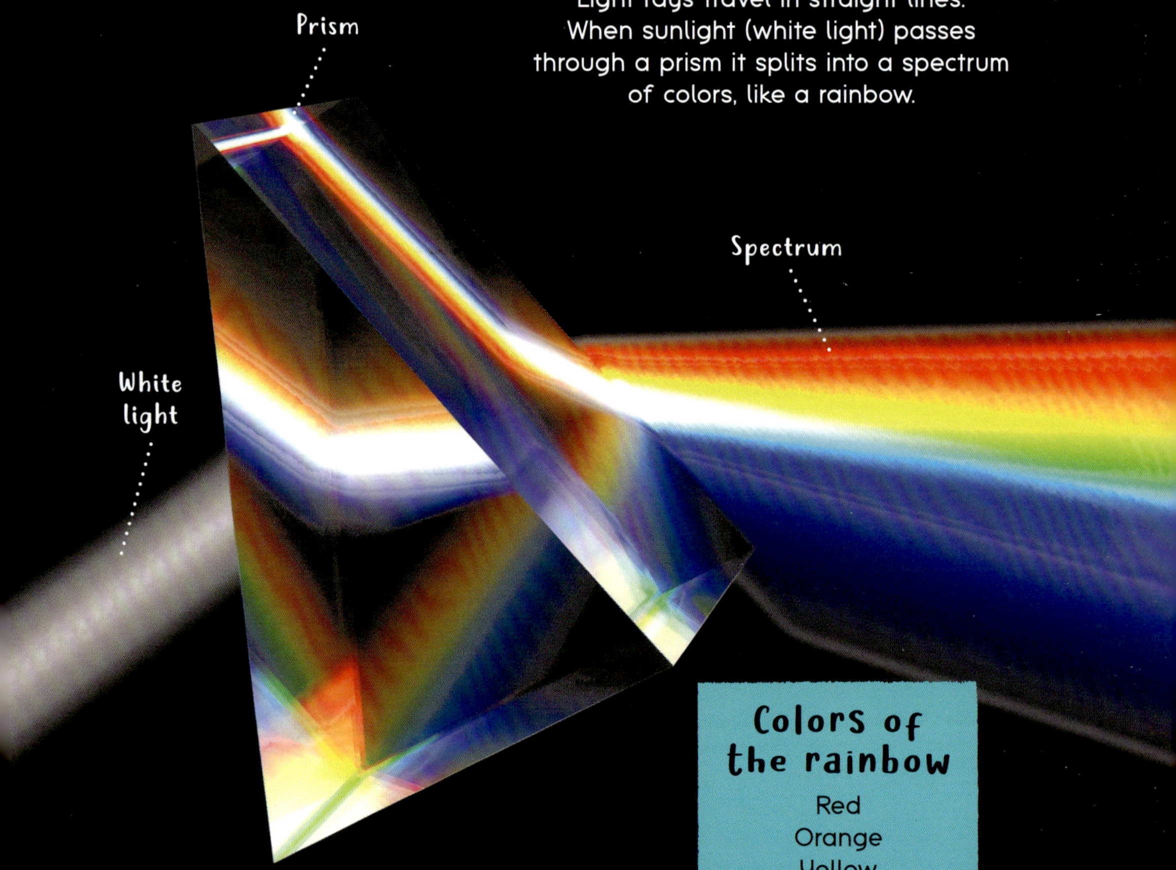

Prism

Spectrum

White light

Colors of the rainbow
Red
Orange
Yellow
Green
Blue
Indigo
Violet

SUPER SCIENCE

Bouncing light

Light rays bounce off surfaces that are smooth, such as a mirror. This is called reflection. If the rays strike at an angle, they may be refracted, or bent.

FUN FACT!
Light is the fastest thing in the Universe. It travels through space at 186,400 miles per second.

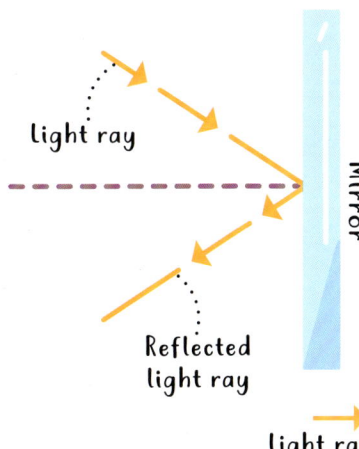

When light rays hit a mirror, almost all of the light is reflected.

If light rays strike the surface at an angle other than 90°, they are refracted.

As light passes through a glass of water, it **refracts** (bends) and makes the straw look bent.

Shades of color

You will need
different-colored paints • gloves apron • paintbrush • pen • paper

1 Put on gloves and an apron and mix two different colors of paint together.

2 Write down what colors you mix and what color they make.

3 Paint a picture using your new colors.

Cameras make pictures by using lenses and light.

57

SUPER SCIENCE

What a noise!

Listening to the radio or television depends on the science of sound. Sounds are carried by invisible waves in the air, which travel about 1,100 feet per second. This is one million times slower than light waves.

Plane taking off 140 dB

Thunder 100 dB

The decibel scale
Scientists measure the loudness of sound in decibels (dB). One of the loudest sounds that we hear is a jet plane engine.

Talking 40 dB

Rustling leaves 10 dB

SUPER SCIENCE

Making the journey

We cannot see sound waves but we can hear them using our ears. Sound waves travel through our ears to our brain.

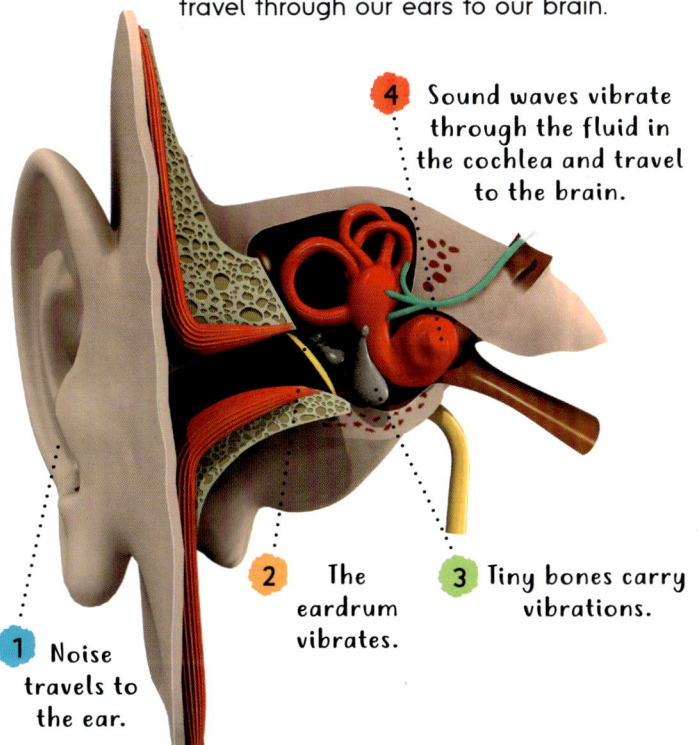

4 Sound waves vibrate through the fluid in the cochlea and travel to the brain.

2 The eardrum vibrates.

3 Tiny bones carry vibrations.

1 Noise travels to the ear.

FUN FACT!

Sound waves bounce off hard, flat surfaces. This is called an echo.

Loudspeakers change electrical signals into sound waves.

When you speak, **sound waves** spread out so everyone can hear what you say.

Box guitar

You will need
shoebox • elastic band • split pins

1. With help from an adult, cut a hole about 4 inches across on one side of an empty shoebox.
2. Push split pins through either side of the hole, and stretch an elastic band between them.
3. Pluck the band. Listen to how the air vibrates inside the box—like a guitar.

SUPER SCIENCE

Magnet power

Magnetism is an invisible force that pulls things together or pushes them apart. Magnets are made from lumps of iron or steel. You can turn a piece of iron into a magnet by stroking it with another magnet.

Magnetic machine
A magnet can also be made by sending electricity through a coil of wire. This is called an electromagnet, and powerful ones are used to recycle metal.

SUPER SCIENCE

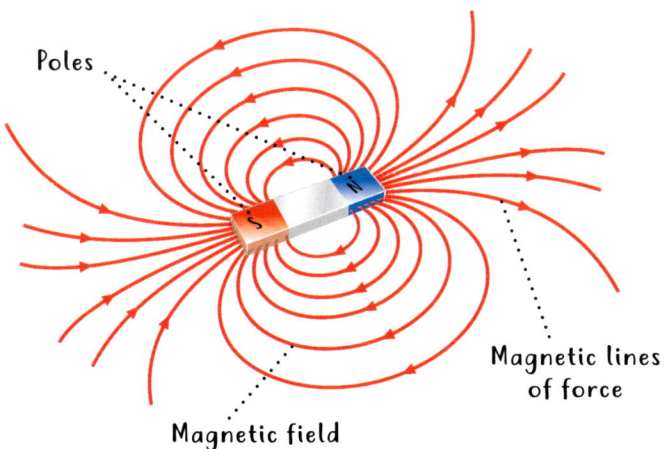

Poles
Magnetic lines of force
Magnetic field

The force of a magnet
A magnet is a block of iron or steel. A force surrounds the magnet, in a region called the magnetic field. The magnetic field is strongest at the two parts of the magnet called the poles.

Floating train
Maglev (magnetic levitation) trains use pushing and pulling magnetic forces to "float" above the track.

A magnet has two different **poles**—north and south.

A car's body is made from **iron-based steel**, which is magnetic.

Some **electromagnets** are so strong they can lift entire cars.

SUPER SCIENCE

What is electricity?

Electricity is energy that flows from a power station to our homes. It is used all around us from power washing machines, and vacuum cleaners, to teakettles. Electricity is made by the movement of electrons inside atoms.

Hopping electrons
When electrons are "pushed," they hop from one atom to the next. This is how electricity flows.

Electron

Atom

Checking cables
Electricity from power plants is carried along cables on high transmission towers. It is very powerful, and extremely dangerous. When cables need to be checked, the electricity is turned off well in advance.

SUPER SCIENCE

Where it comes from
A power plant makes enough electricity for thousands of homes.

Generator

Cables

Transmission tower

Solar panels can make electricity from the Sun's light energy.

A **battery** makes electricity from different chemicals, such as an acid and a metal, swapping electrons.

Transmission towers hold cables safely above the ground.

Make a circuit

You will need
lightbulb • battery • wire

1. Ask an adult to help. Join a bulb to a battery with pieces of wire, as shown.
2. Electricity flows in a circuit (loop) from the battery and through the wires to the lightbulb, and lights the bulb.

SUPER SCIENCE

Mighty materials

You would not make a bridge out of straw, or a cup out of thin paper. Choosing the right material is important. Cars are made from tough, long-lasting materials. Metal, plastic, and rubber are all materials used to make cars.

The right substances
A racing car has thousands of parts made from hundreds of materials. Many parts need to be strong, but not weigh much, so the car can go as fast as possible.

The engine is very powerful, but also needs to be light.

The main body of the car is made from carbon fiber. It is strong and light, and protects the car from damage.

SUPER SCIENCE

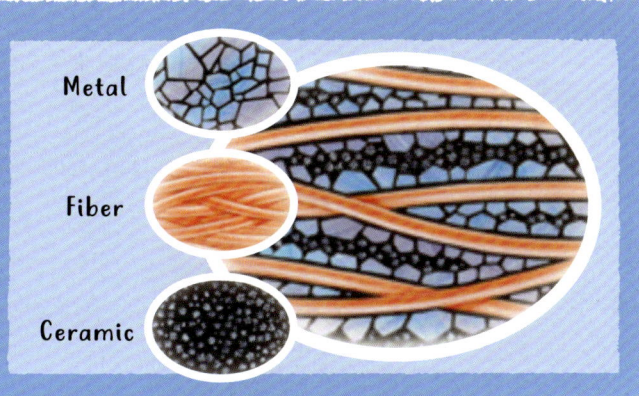

Clever composites

Metal, fiber, and ceramic can combine to make a composite material. The ways these elements are arranged can affect the composite's strength.

Made by nature

Many materials come from plants. Wood comes from the trunks and branches of trees. Cotton comes from the seeds of cotton plants to make clothes such as t-shirts.

Plastics are mainly made from oil. We should recycle plastic where possible.

Ceramics are made from clay that is dug from the earth.

Glass is made from limestone and sand.

SUPER SCIENCE

Mini Science

Everything in the world is made of atoms. Atoms are the smallest bits of a substance. They are so tiny that even a billion atoms would be too small to see.

Looking inside
Inside an atom are even smaller bits called subatomic particles. There are three main kinds—protons, neutrons, and electrons.

Inside an atom

1. The center of the atom is called the nucleus. It contains protons (red), and neutrons (blue).
2. Around the center of each atom are subatomic particles called electrons. They whizz round the nucleus.
3. On this illustration, paths indicate the movement of electrons around the nucleus.

SUPER SCIENCE

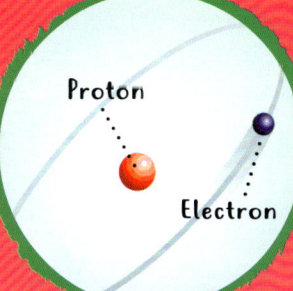

Hydrogen is a gas with just one proton.

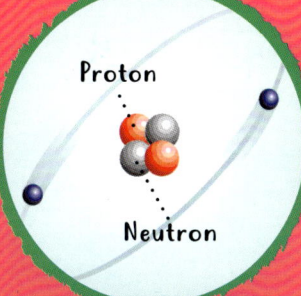

Helium is a gas with two protons and two neutrons.

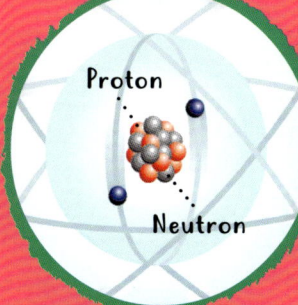

Oxygen, the gas we need to breathe, has eight protons and eight neutrons.

FUN FACT!

Atoms are so small that a grain of sand contains at least 100 billion billion of them!

DEADLY DINOSAURS

What are dinosaurs?

Dinosaurs were reptiles—a group of animals with scaly skin that lived millions of years ago. There were many different kinds of dinosaurs, but they all died out long, long ago.

Sharp teeth

Small arms

Powerful legs

The tyrannosaurs
Gorgosaurus belonged to the tyrannosaur group of dinosaurs, along with *T-Rex*. It was 26–30 feet long. Tyrannosaurs had hollow bones to make them lighter.

DEADLY DINOSAURS

Before *T-Rex*
Guanlong is known as "crown dragon" because it had a horn-like plate of bone on its nose. It was around nearly 100 million years before *Tyrannosaurus rex*.

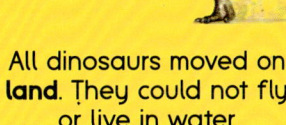

All dinosaurs moved on **land**. They could not fly or live in water.

Famous dinosaur
Tyrannosaurus rex is the most well-known fearsome dinosaur. When eating large prey, it would tear the flesh, gulp it in lumps, and swallow it whole.

We can learn about dinosaurs through their remains, or **fossils**.

Some **dinosaurs** were plant-eaters, while others ate meat.

DEADLY DINOSAURS

The Age of Dinosaurs

Dinosaurs lived between 230 million and 66 million years ago. This vast length of time is called the Mesozoic Era, or the Age of Dinosaurs. The Mesozoic Era was split into three time periods—the Triassic, Jurassic, and Cretaceous.

Triassic Period 252–201 million years ago

Dinosaurs first appeared in the Triassic Period. Fossils of the earliest dinosaurs are from the mid-Triassic Period, about 230 million years ago. Around the end of the Triassic Period, dinosaurs became much stronger, as they could stand upright, on two feet.

DEADLY DINOSAURS

Jurassic Period 201–145 million years ago

During the Jurassic Period, dinosaurs reached their greatest size and spread around the world. The biggest dinosaurs were the sauropods, or "lizard feet." Long-necked herbivores were hunted by powerful carnivores.

Cretaceous Period 145–66 million years ago

Many different types of dinosaurs developed during the Cretaceous Period. Thousands of fossils from this period have been discovered, such as the small but deadly carnivore, *Deinonychus*.

Standing on **two feet** meant the dinosaurs could run faster and further.

When the dinosaurs died out, **mammals** became the main land animals.

FUN FACT!

The word dinosaur means "terrible lizard." However, dinosaurs weren't really lizards, and not all of them were terrible!

Gentle giants

Sauropods were dinosaur giants. These enormous creatures all had small heads, long necks, long tails, barrel-shaped bodies, and four legs.

Towering above
Long necks enabled most sauropods to chomp on plant matter high in trees. Others preferred to graze on low growing plants.

Diplodocus

Brachiosaurus

DEADLY DINOSAURS

Size and scale
Some of the biggest sauropods were *Brachiosaurus*, *Argentinosaurus* and *Apatosaurus*. This scale shows how big they were compared to an adult human.

Apatosaurus was 75 feet long. Its tail had 82 bones and was used to whip enemies.

Brachiosaurus was 82 feet long. With its long front legs and neck, it could reach food 45 feet from the ground.

FUN FACT!
Diplodocus is also known as "Old Whip-tail!" It could swish its long tail so hard and fast that it made an enormous CRACK like a whip.

Brachiosaurus had peglike teeth for raking leaves.

Sauropods had claws that were almost flat. Some even looked like they had toenails!

Biggest of all
Argentinosaurus was the biggest sauropod at 130 feet in length and 110 tons in weight.

73

DEADLY DINOSAURS

Huge hunters

The biggest meat-eating dinosaurs were the largest hunters ever to have lived. Different types came and went during the Age of Dinosaurs. One of the largest hunters was *Tyrannosaurus rex*.

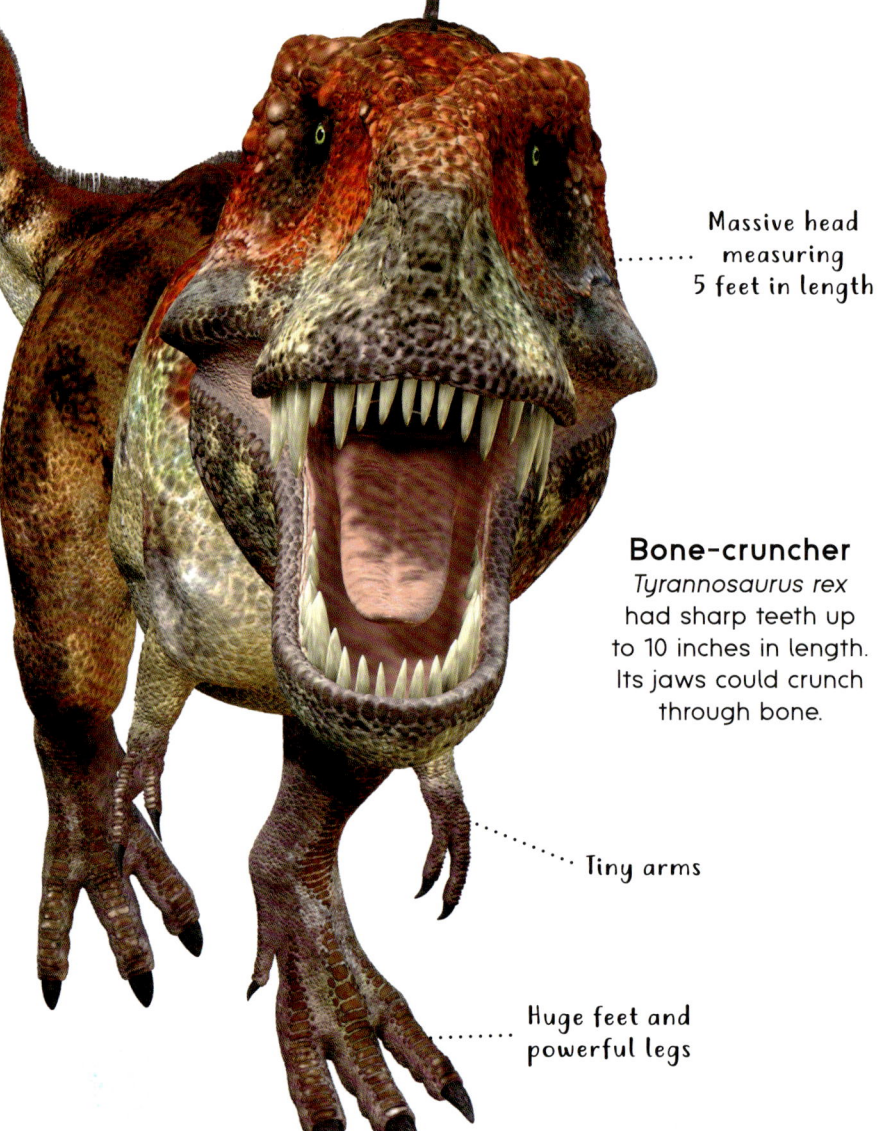

Massive head measuring 5 feet in length

Bone-cruncher
Tyrannosaurus rex had sharp teeth up to 10 inches in length. Its jaws could crunch through bone.

Tiny arms

Huge feet and powerful legs

DEADLY DINOSAURS

Built for hunting
Predators like *T-Rex* had strong legs for running, and giant toe claws for kicking and holding down victims.

Giganotosaurus had three clawed fingers on each hand.

Powerful predator
Allosaurus was a big, fast-moving hunter with powerful jaws. It lived millions of years before *T-Rex*.

- Long tail
- Eyebrow horns
- Powerful jaws with long teeth
- Sharp-clawed hands
- Long, strong legs and clawed feet

Spinosaurus is the biggest meat-eating animal that has ever lived.

FUN FACT!
Some meat-eating dinosaurs not only bit their prey, but also each other! Fossils of several tyrannosaurs had bite marks on their heads.

DEADLY DINOSAURS

Eggs and nests

Like most reptiles today, dinosaurs produced young by laying eggs. These hatched out into baby dinosaurs that gradually grew into adults. Fossils have been found of eggs with dinosaurs still developing inside, as well as fossils of newly hatched baby dinosaurs.

Sitting on eggs
It is now thought that some dinosaurs, like this *Citipati*, actually built nests and incubated their eggs.

Protecting eggs
Oviraptor laid its eggs in circles inside a bowl-shaped nest in the ground. The mother protected its eggs from hungry hunters.

DEADLY DINOSAURS

FUN FACT!
T-Rex laid sausage-shaped eggs that were 15 inches long and 6 inches wide. It probably didn't look after its young.

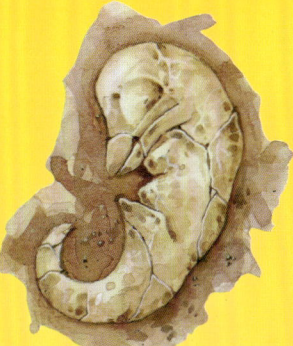

A **fossilized embryo** developing inside an egg.

Dinosaur eggs were **leathery and bendy**, like reptile eggs today.

DEADLY DINOSAURS

Caring parents

Some dinosaurs, like *Maiasaura*, may have cared for their babies and brought food to the nest.

Fossils of *Maiasaura* include nests, eggs, newly hatched young, and broken eggshells.

Fully formed baby fills the space inside egg.

Tiny embryo is nourished by yolk.

Developing embryo.

DEADLY DINOSAURS

Maiasaura bringing food to young.

Hatchling

Iguanodon adults protected their young by keeping them in the middle of the herd.

Most **baby dinosaurs** had to fend for themselves after hatching.

FUN FACT!
Baby dinosaurs grew up to five times faster than human babies. Some were already 3 feet long when they hatched!

DEADLY DINOSAURS

Where did they go?

Dinosaurs died out 66 million years ago. There are dinosaur fossils in rocks up to this time, but none after this. However, there are fossils of creatures such as fish and mammals. Perhaps a giant rock (meteorite) from space smashed into Earth, killing the dinosaurs.

DEADLY DINOSAURS

Deadly meteorite
A meteorite would have thrown up clouds of ash and dust, blocking out the Sun. Plants would have died, leaving no food for the plant-eating dinosaurs. When the plant-eaters died, the meat-eating dinosaurs would have starved.

Other animals may have eaten all the dinosaur eggs.

FUN FACT!
Dinosaurs may have been killed by a disease. It could have spread among all the dinosaurs and killed them off.

Erupting volcanoes
Volcanoes around Earth could have erupted at the same time. This would have thrown out red-hot rocks, ash, dust, and clouds of poisonous gas. Dinosaurs would have choked and died in the gloom.

A **giant wave** may have drowned the dinosaurs.

FANTASTIC MAMMALS

What are mammals?

There are thousands of mammals living on Earth. Some can swim, some can fly, and all are warm-blooded. Being warm-blooded means that mammals can keep their body temperature the same in any weather conditions.

In the ocean
There are more than 35 different kinds of dolphins. The dusky dolphin likes to swim near boats, and can leap and somersault above the waves.

FUN FACT!
Dolphins can travel and feed in groups of up to 2,000!

FANTASTIC MAMMALS

Elephants on parade

You will need
paper • pens • scissors

1. Fold a long sheet of paper backward and forward into wide zigzags.
2. Draw an elephant shape onto the top page, with the tail joined to one edge and the trunk to the other.
3. With help from an adult, cut around the outline.
4. Draw ears and eyes onto each shape and color them in. Open out your chain. All the elephants are holding trunks and tails!

Caring for young

Orangutans are the largest mammals to live in trees. Like all mammals, young orangutans feed on their mother's milk.

Pangolins are covered in hard scales for protection.

Red pandas sleep during the day and feed at night.

Beavers have flat tails and webbed feet, making them excellent swimmers.

FANTASTIC MAMMALS

Mammal families

Some mammals live alone, except for when they have young. Other mammals like to live in groups. There are different names for these groups, depending on the animal.

FANTASTIC MAMMALS

A troop of chimps

A pack of wolves

A harem of seals

A coterie of prairie dogs

Group names
Mammal groups are often given names that we call collective nouns. Can you think of any more?

Lions live in groups called **prides**. All other big cats live alone.

Koalas live alone in trees. They eat the leaves of eucalyptus plants.

Meerkats live in large groups called colonies of up to 30 animals.

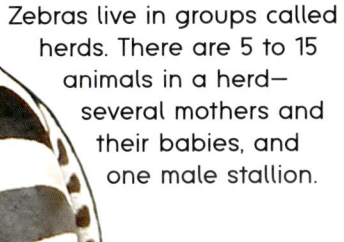

Striped herd
Zebras live in groups called herds. There are 5 to 15 animals in a herd—several mothers and their babies, and one male stallion.

FANTASTIC MAMMALS

Big and Small

The blue whale is the biggest mammal, and animal, in the world. This ocean giant measures up to 110 feet in length—as long as seven family cars parked end to end. The biggest land mammal is the elephant, while the smallest is the hog-nosed bat.

Land giant
Elephants are the biggest animals to live on land. African elephants can reach 6.5 tons in weight and stand 13 feet tall at the shoulder.

FANTASTIC MAMMALS

Great giant
The blue whale is a true giant. It reaches up to 165 tons in weight—that's as heavy as 2,000 people or 35 elephants!

Chevrotains are the smallest deer—they are the size of hares.

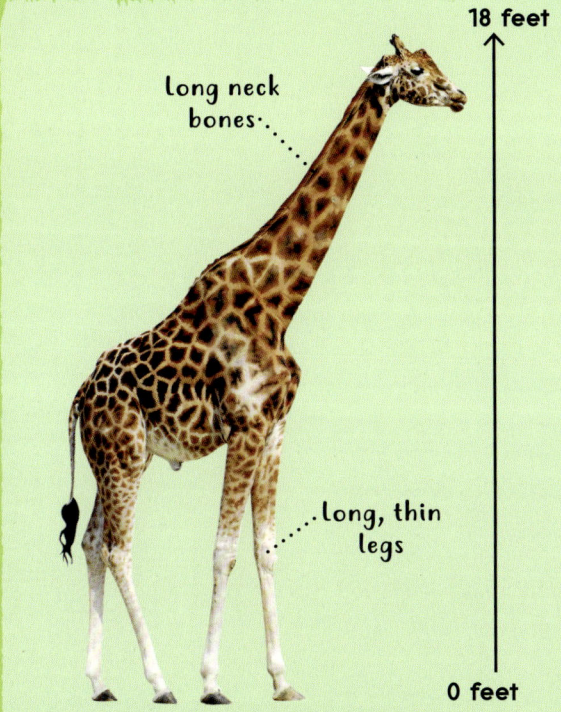

18 feet

long neck bones

long, thin legs

0 feet

Towering above
The giraffe is the tallest of all mammals. It reaches 18 feet in height—the same as three people standing on each other's shoulders.

Capybaras are the largest rodents in the world.

Pygmy shrews have such small eyes, they rely on their senses of smell and hearing.

Plant food

Plant-eaters spend much of their time eating in order to get enough nourishment (goodness from food). A good thing about being a plant-eater is that the animal does not have to chase and fight for its food as hunters do.

Bamboo lover
Nearly all of the panda's diet is bamboo. It eats fresh shoots in spring, mature leaves in summer, and stems in winter.

FANTASTIC MAMMALS

Long tongue
The giraffe's black tongue is almost 12 inches long. It uses it to grip leaves and pull them into its mouth.

Rabbits have strong teeth for eating tough plants and bark.

Munching lemurs
Lemurs mainly eat plants. They live in tropical forests where there are lots of fresh leaves and ripe fruit all year round.

Rhinos can be heard munching on plants from 440 yards away.

Wombats feed on the grass around their burrow.

FANTASTIC MAMMALS

Hungry hunters

Mammals that hunt and kill other creatures are called carnivores. Lions, tigers, wolves, and dogs are all carnivores. Many carnivores do not have to hunt every day—one kill will last them for several days.

Meat and plants
Bears are carnivores, but many eat more plants than meat. In summer, brown bears wade into rivers and catch fish.

FANTASTIC MAMMALS

Practice makes perfect
The lion is an expert hunter. Creeping up on its prey, such as deer, it pounces and kills its victim quickly.

Wolves hunt in packs, so they can kill larger animals.

A pack of **hunting dogs** will try to separate one animal from the rest of its herd.

Tigers are perfectly camouflaged to hide from their prey.

Cool cats!

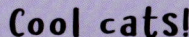

You will need
scissors • paper plate • paints • paintbrush
glue • paper • wool • elastic bands

1. With help from an adult, cut eye and nose holes in the plate.
2. Paint a cat face—maybe a tiger or a lion.
3. Stick on paper ears and whiskers, and a mane made from wool.
4. Make a hole through each side of the plate and loop elastic bands through the holes. Slip the bands over your ears and roar away!

River mammals

Most river mammals spend only part of their time in water. Creatures such as the otter and water rat live on land, and go into the water to find food. The hippopotamus, however, spends most of its day in water to keep cool.

Strong swimmer
Otters have webbed paws to help them swim fast to hunt for prey such as fish.

In the depths
The platypus uses its ducklike beak to find food in the murky riverbed. It has webbed feet to help it swim through the water.

FANTASTIC MAMMALS

Strong Swimmer
The water opossum is perfectly adapted for the water. It has waterproof fur, and its strong, webbed back feet help it to swim with ease.

FUN FACT!
The duck-billed platypus is an Australian egg-laying mammal. Males have poisonous stingers on their back feet to keep potential predators at bay.

Manatees are water-living mammals that feed on plants.

Hippos are not good swimmers. Instead, they walk on the riverbed.

FANTASTIC MAMMALS

Snow mammals

Mammals that live in very cold places, such as the Arctic and Antarctic, have thick fur to keep them warm. The color of their fur is very important as it helps them to hide in the snow.

FUN FACT!
Polar bears have thick fur to keep out the Arctic cold—even the soles of their feet are furry!

Arctic hunter
The polar bear is the biggest land mammal in the Arctic. It can run fast, swim well, and even dive under the ice to hunt its main prey—seals.

FANTASTIC MAMMALS

Thick coat
The snow leopard lives in the mountains of central Asia. It has thick fur to keep it warm in the freezing conditions.

White pups
Harp seal pups are born on the Arctic ice, where they are fed by their mothers. Their white coats help them to hide from hungry polar bears.

Male walruses have long teeth, called tusks, for digging up shellfish from the seabed.

Musk oxen have long, shaggy fur to help them to survive the Arctic cold.

Snowshoe hares have brown coats in summer, which then turn white in winter.

FANTASTIC MAMMALS

Fins and flippers

Most swimming mammals have fins and flippers instead of legs. Seals and sea lions have paddlelike flippers. They use them to drag themselves along on land, as well as for swimming. Whales and dolphins never come onto land. They use their tails and flippers to swim.

Strong flippers
These Australian sea lions are built for swimming, but their long, strong flippers help them move quickly on land, too.

FANTASTIC MAMMALS

Graceful swimmers
Seals are brilliant swimmers. They have smaller flippers than sea lions, and lack the visible ear flaps that sea lions have.

The **gray whale** dives to the seafloor to feed using filters in its mouth called baleen.

Flipper

Amazing acrobatics
Humpback whales can weigh up to 33 tons, but they are able to leap out of the water using their powerful flippers and tail.

Dolphins can often be seen leaping from the water.

Killer whales are the largest members of the dolphin family.

97

FANTASTIC MAMMALS

In the rain forest

Rain forest mammals live at all levels of the forest, from the tallest trees to the forest floor. Bats fly over treetops, and monkeys and apes swing from branches. Lower down, smaller creatures such as civets and pottos hide among the thick greenery.

Down in the swamp
Jaguars live in the rain forests of Central and South America. They are strong swimmers, and can often be found in swampy areas.

FANTASTIC MAMMALS

Tops of the trees
The aye-aye is related to the lemur. It has an unusually long middle finger, so it can dig into trees and pull out grubs to eat.

Tapirs live on the rain forest floor and have long, bendy snouts.

Moving around
Ring-tailed lemurs only live on the island of Madagascar. In the rain forest, they walk along the ground and move through the trees.

Agoutis have strong teeth that can bite through hard nut shells.

FUN FACT!
Tapirs are very good swimmers. They use their snout, which can move and grasp things in a similar way to an elephant's trunk, as a snorkel.

FANTASTIC MAMMALS

Desert life

Mammals that live in the desert have developed ways to escape the scorching heat. The North African gerbil burrows underground and only comes out at night. Not all deserts are hot—the Gobi Desert in Asia can be cold during winter.

Keeping warm
The camel has thick fur to keep it warm during the Gobi Desert's cold winter.

FANTASTIC MAMMALS

The **desert kangaroo rat** comes out at night to find seeds.

Hyenas are good hunters, and sometimes steal other animals' food.

Finding water
Wildebeest find areas where there is enough water to drink.

FUN FACT!
Desert-dwelling elephants may travel long distances every day to search for water. They survive by eating plants that are full of moisture if water is scarce.

Fennec foxes have large ears to help them lose heat.

BRILLIANT BIRDS

What is a bird?

All birds have two legs, a pair of wings, and a body that is covered in feathers. Birds live all over the world, from icy Antarctica to the hottest deserts.

Safe and sound
All birds lay eggs with a hard shell. This protects the growing young. The parent birds keep the eggs safe and warm until the chicks hatch.

New life
Once the chicks hatch from their eggs, they need to be fed regularly to help them grow stronger.

BRILLIANT BIRDS

Crown

Bill or beak

Breast

Back

Wing

Legs

Claw

Tail

Feet

Made for flight
A bird's body is designed to help it fly. It has light, hollow bones and special flight feathers on its wings.

Whistling swans are thought to have the most feathers of any bird— more than 25,000.

Ostriches have strong legs so they can run fast.

Hornbills have hornlike growths on their beaks called casques.

Take off
Pigeons have strong wing muscles that help them to take off quickly and fly at speeds of up to 50 miles an hour.

BRILLIANT BIRDS

Starting life

A bird's egg protects the chick growing inside. The yolk provides food, while layers of egg white cushion the chick. The shell is hard but porous—it allows air in and out so the chick can breathe.

Time to hatch
When it is ready to hatch, the chick chips away at the eggshell and breaks free.

1 The chick starts to crack the egg.

Escape tools
An egg tooth is a small, sharp lump on a chick's beak that helps it to break the eggshell when it is time to hatch.

2 The chick uses its egg tooth to break the shell.

3 The egg splits wide open.

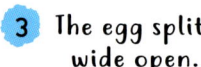

4 The chick is able to wriggle free. Its parents will look after it for several weeks until it can care for itself.

BRILLIANT BIRDS

On a cliff
Guillemots live on clifftops. They do not build nests, but simply lay their eggs on the rock or bare earth.

Keeping eggs warm
Parent birds, such as the emu, take turns to sit on the eggs to keep them warm. This is called incubation.

Baby geese are called **goslings**, and they can swim soon after they've hatched.

Emperor penguins only lay a single egg each year. Rearing a chick in the harsh Antarctic environment is tough.

FUN FACT!
The guillemot's egg is pear-shaped, so that if the egg is pushed or knocked, it does not roll off the cliff.

BRILLIANT BIRDS

Bird homes

Birds make nests in which to lay their eggs and keep them safe. Nests can be made of twigs, leaves, mud, or saliva. They are built in a variety of places, such as trees, near water, or in the walls of buildings.

Big nest
The bald eagle makes one of the biggest nests of any bird. It is made of sticks and built in a tree or on rocks.

FUN FACT!
The cave swiflet uses its own saliva to stick grass and feathers together.

BRILLIANT BIRDS

Hanging home
The male weaver bird makes a nest from grass and stems. He knots and weaves the pieces together to make a long nest, which hangs from the branch of a tree.

1. The male weaver bird twists strips of leaves around a branch or twig.

2. Then he makes a roof and an entrance.

3. When the nest is finished, the long entrance helps to provide a safe shelter for the eggs.

Woodpeckers drill a hole in a tree in which to make their nests.

Magellanic penguins nest in bushes, burrows, or caves in South America.

Black-browed albatrosses make a simple nest on open cliffs.

BRILLIANT BIRDS

Fast fliers

The fastest flying bird is the peregrine falcon. It hunts other birds in the air and makes amazing high-speed dives to catch its prey. Ducks and geese are also fast fliers. The eider duck can reach speeds of more than 60 miles an hour.

Powerful hunter
A peregrine falcon can reach speeds of 110 miles an hour when hunting.

BRILLIANT BIRDS

Make a bird cake

You will need
8 oz of suet, lard, or fat drippings • 1 lb of seeds or nuts • empty clay pot • string • pan

1. Ask an adult for help. Melt the fat in a pan on a low heat and mix it with the seeds or nuts.
2. Pour the mixture into the clay pot and leave it to cool.
3. Remove the cake from the pot. Make a hole through the cake and put a string through the hole. Hang it from a tree outside and watch the birds eat the yummy treat!

Mute swans can fly at over 50 miles an hour during migration.

Mallard ducks are fast fliers, and can reach speeds of 55 miles an hour.

Swallows twist and zigzag in the air as they fly.

Beating wings
Hummingbirds beat their wings more than 50 times a second as they hover in the air.

BRILLIANT BIRDS

Swimmers and divers

Penguins are the best swimmers and divers in the bird world. They spend most of their lives in water, using their wings as strong flippers to help them swim.

Built to swim
Like all penguins, these king penguins are brilliant swimmers. Their torpedo-shaped bodies help to propel them through the water.

FUN FACT!
The gentoo penguin is one of the fastest swimming birds. It can swim faster than most people can run!

BRILLIANT BIRDS

Short dives
Arctic terns catch fish and other creatures by making short dives into the water.

Kingfishers plunge into rivers to grab fish with daggerlike beaks.

Northern gannets dive from great heights to catch fish from the sea.

Upside down
Some types of duck find food by turning themselves upside down to search under the surface of the water.

Ospreys are skilled at plucking fish from the water.

BRILLIANT BIRDS

Night birds

Some birds hunt at night, when there is less competition for prey. These birds have special ways of finding their way in the dark. They might have a strong sense of smell or sensitive eyesight.

Roly-poly owl!

You will need
scissors • empty plastic tub • drinking straw
empty cotton spool • colored paper • glue

1 With help from an adult, make two small holes at the top of the plastic tub. Push a drinking straw through one side of the tub, through the center of the cotton reel and out through the other hole.

2 Cut out eyes, wings, and a beak from colored paper and stick them onto the tub. Now roll your owl around!

BRILLIANT BIRDS

Poorwills hunt at night by opening their beaks wide to snap insects from the air.

Male nightingales sing regularly after sunset to attract females.

Kiwis have a good sense of smell, which helps them to find food.

Strong senses
Barn owls have large, sensitive eyes to help them see in the dark. They also have very good hearing.

113

BRILLIANT BIRDS

Feeding time

All birds have a beak for eating. They have different kinds of beak, suited to the types of food they eat. Insect-eating birds have thin, sharp beaks for picking up tiny prey. Hunting birds have hooked beaks for tearing flesh.

Eating insects
The European bee-eater uses its sharp beak to catch bees, wasps, and dragonflies. Once it has snapped up an insect, it rubs its catch on a branch to get rid of the sting.

Eggs for dinner
The Egyptian vulture steals other birds' eggs. It cracks the eggs by dropping them on the ground or by dropping stones on them.

BRILLIANT BIRDS

Hummingbirds use their long, thin beaks to reach flower nectar.

A nutty treat
Nuthatches feed on nuts and seeds as well as some insects. They have a long, pointed beak and can hang upside down so they can easily get at food.

Vultures and marabou storks have bald heads so they don't get messy scavenging in carcasses.

Fish food
Puffins have large colorful beaks that can hold 12 or more fish. This allows them to fill their beaks and carry food back to their young.

Oxpeckers pull ticks from the skin of animals such as antelopes.

BRILLIANT BIRDS

Fierce hunters

Eagles, hawks, and owls are birds of prey—they hunt other animals. All have keen senses, muscular bodies, large bills, and sharp talons. They are also called raptors, which means to grab, as they kill with their feet.

Hunting snakes
Secretary birds are not like other birds of prey. They hunt snakes by stamping on them using their long, powerful legs.

Food on the wing
Philippine eagles hunt from perches. They eat lots of different animals, such as flying lemurs, monkeys, bats, and snakes. Philippine eagles are very rare, and they are protected by law.

BRILLIANT BIRDS

Like all birds of prey, **buzzards** use their hooked bill and sharp talons to rip prey apart.

The **Andean condor** is the biggest bird of prey. Its wingspan can reach 10 feet in males.

Use your feet!

You will need
different sized objects such as pencils, coins, and books

1. Get your friends together to see if you can pick things up using your feet—just like an eagle.
2. Start with the easiest object, such as a pencil. Make the objects harder and harder to pick up with your feet. Whoever can pick up the most objects is the winner!

Hawks can be helpful to humans because they hunt rodents that damage crops.

AWESOME BUGS

What is a bug?

If a creepy-crawly has six legs, it is an insect. If it has more legs or none at all, then it is another kind of animal. The young of some insects have no legs until they become adults.

Insect features
This stag beetle has six legs and a body divided into three parts, so it is an insect.

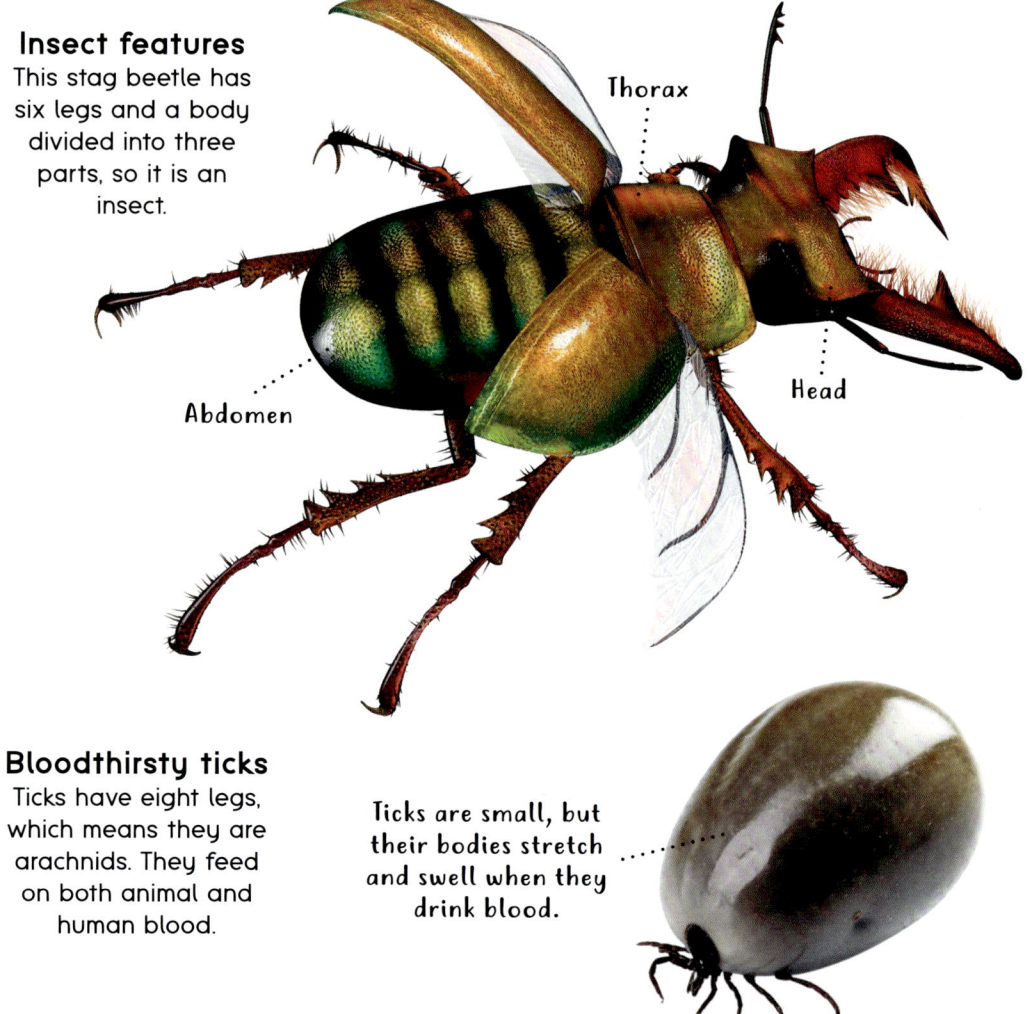

Thorax

Head

Abdomen

Bloodthirsty ticks
Ticks have eight legs, which means they are arachnids. They feed on both animal and human blood.

Ticks are small, but their bodies stretch and swell when they drink blood.

AWESOME BUGS

Hundreds of legs
Millipedes are myriapods. They may have hundreds of pairs of legs and their bodies are long and segmented.

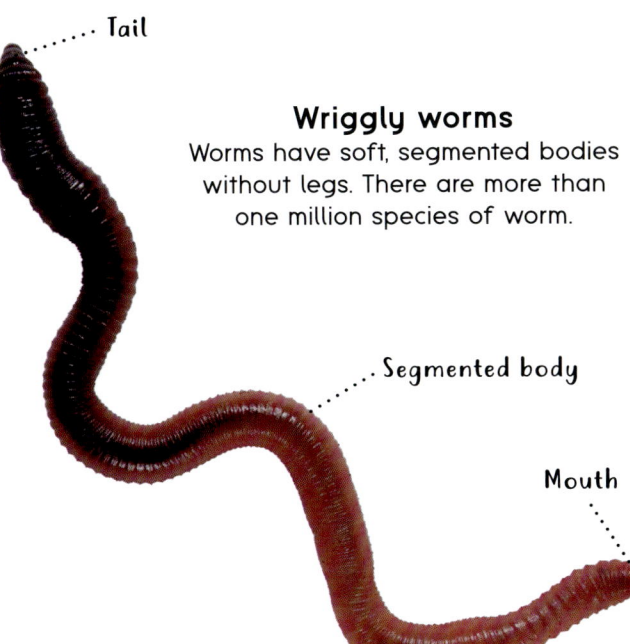

..... Tail

Wriggly worms
Worms have soft, segmented bodies without legs. There are more than one million species of worm.

..... Segmented body

Mouth .....

Snails are mollusks. They have hard shells to protect their soft bodies.

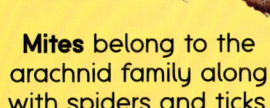

Mites belong to the arachnid family along with spiders and ticks.

Centipedes are also myriapods. They have a poisonous bite to kill prey.

AWESOME BUGS

The insect world

Insects form the largest of all animal groups, with millions of different kinds, or species. They are found almost everywhere in the world. Common insects include flies, ladybugs, butterflies, ants, and bees.

Making honey
Honeybees live in nests called hives. They share jobs such as finding food, cleaning the nest, and caring for young.

Butterfly life cycle
Butterflies go through a life cycle called metamorphosis, changing from egg to caterpillar to chrysalis to adult.

A bees' nest has hundreds of six-sided holes with wax walls.

AWESOME BUGS

FUN FACT!
As bees collect pollen, they spread it from flower to flower, to make new seeds. If there were fewer bees, there would be fewer flowers.

Some holes in the nest contain honey the bees have made from flower nectar and pollen.

Other holes contain larvae, which the adult bees feed and care for.

Cockchafer beetles can be found in woodland, farmland, and gardens.

Male **scorpionflies** have a harmless sting on a long, curved tail.

Earwigs live in dark, damp corners. They are mostly active at night.

AWESOME BUGS

Taking flight

Many insects can fly. The wings are attached to the middle part of their body, called the thorax. Most insects have two pairs of wings.

The hard outer wings are called elytra. They are red with black spots.

The outer wings part to reveal the soft, flying wings underneath.

Special wings
Ladybugs fly using their soft inner wings. They fly to look for food, to find new homes, and to escape danger.

AWESOME BUGS

Up and away!

You will need
sticky tape • tissue paper
stiff card (heavy paper)

1. Carefully fold the stiff card to make a cube-shaped box with two open ends.
2. Attach strips of stiff card to the sides to make struts for the wings. Make the wings from tissue paper and attach to the main box and the struts.
3. Hold the box as shown. Move the top and bottom walls in, then out. This bends the side walls to make the wings flap.

Apollo butterflies are strong fliers. They can fly to the top of mountains.

FUN FACT!
The heaviest flying insect is the Goliath beetle. These huge insects are as big as a human hand!

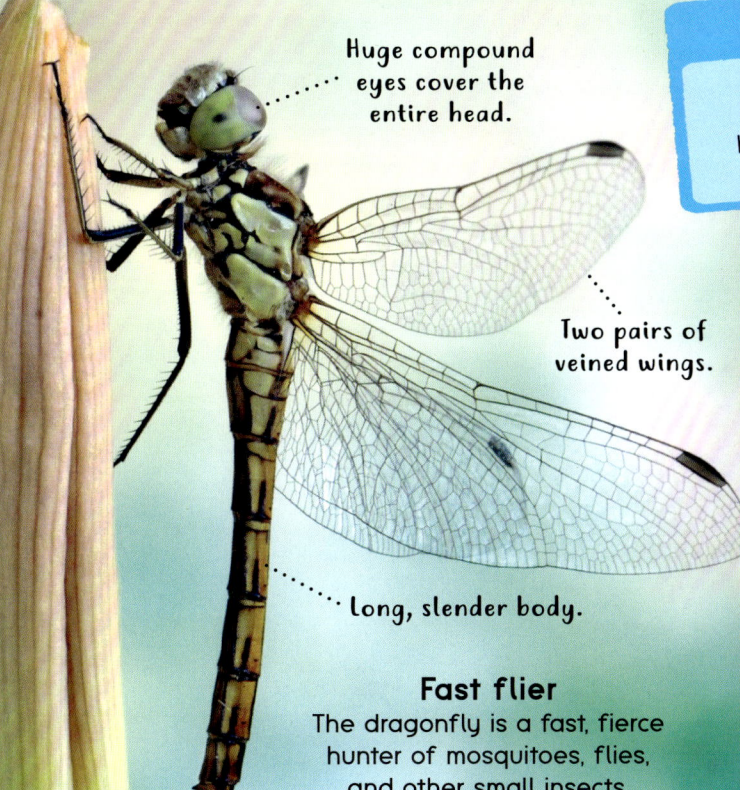

Huge compound eyes cover the entire head.

Two pairs of veined wings.

Long, slender body.

Fast flier
The dragonfly is a fast, fierce hunter of mosquitoes, flies, and other small insects.

Hummingbird hawk-moths hover like hummingbirds to drink from flowers.

AWESOME BUGS

Attack and defend

Insects may be small, but they are also fierce. Many have mouthparts shaped like spears or saws, for grabbing and tearing up prey. Some have deadly bites and stings. Others have clever defenses against predators.

FUN FACT!
A female praying mantis isn't fussy about what she eats. She will sometimes eat her male mate after or even during mating!

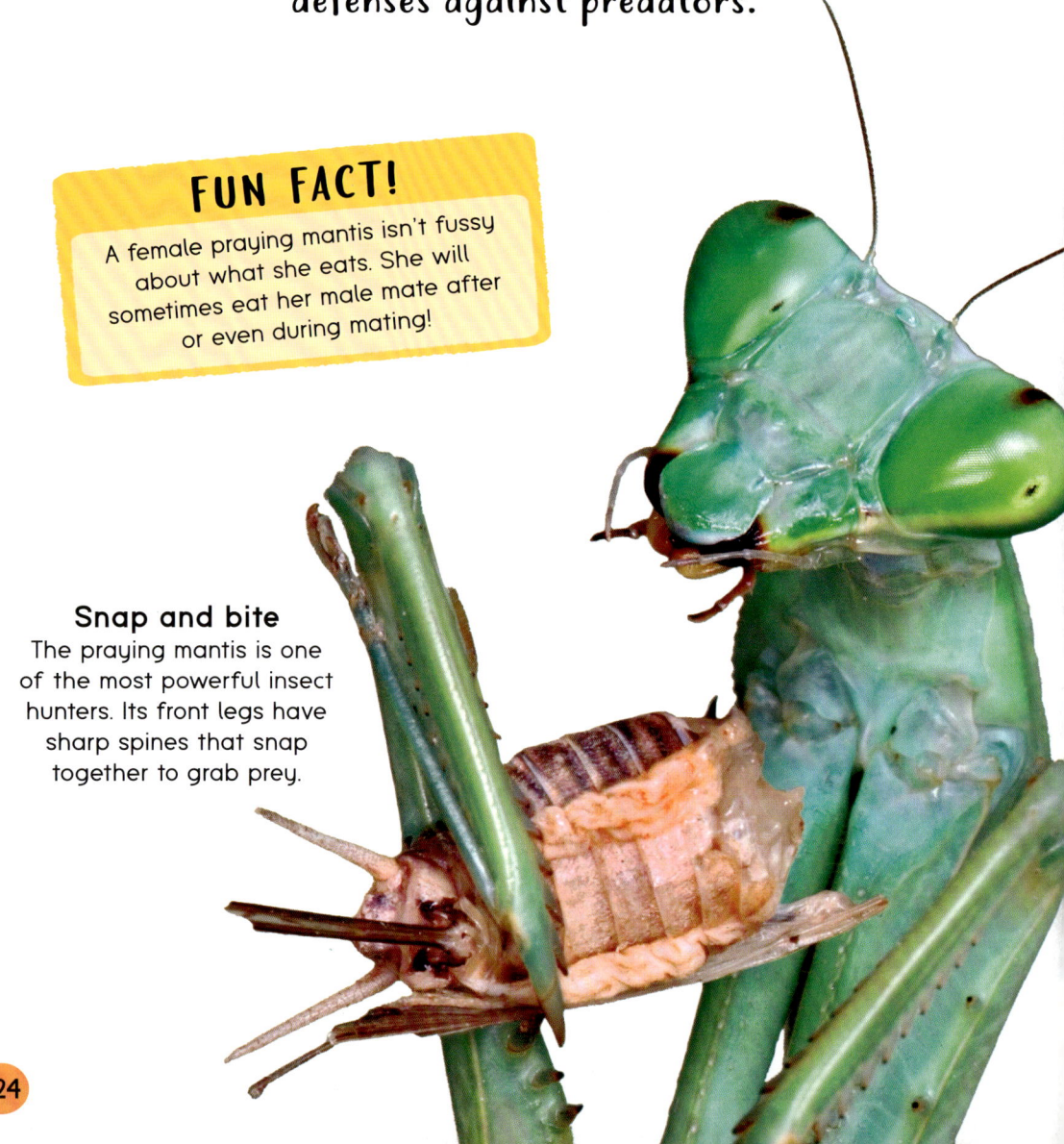

Snap and bite
The praying mantis is one of the most powerful insect hunters. Its front legs have sharp spines that snap together to grab prey.

AWESOME BUGS

Pierce and paralyze
The red-banded sand wasp uses its strong jaws to pierce its prey's thin skin. It then injects poison to paralyze its victim.

Toxic defense
Bombardier beetles can squirt a boiling, foul-smelling spray to defend themselves against predators.

This **caterpillar** looks like bird droppings to avoid being eaten by predators.

Bullet ants have the most painful sting in the insect world. They live in South American jungles.

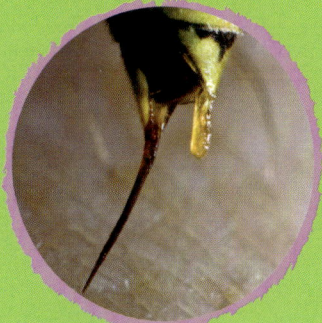

Hornets are a type of large wasp with very painful stings.

Hide and Seek

Many insects are colored or patterned to blend in with their natural surroundings. This is called "camouflage." It helps insects hide from hunters and allows predators to sneak up on prey, unseen.

Hard to spot
Stick insects are excellent at camouflaging themselves, especially when they keep still or sway with the wind.

Walking leaves
Leaf insects are leafy-green in color and are very hard to spot among foliage.

AWESOME BUGS

Now you See me...

You will need
heavy paper • cardboard • glue • coloring pens • scissors

1. With help from an adult, cut out a butterfly shape from heavy paper. Color it brightly.
2. Next, cut out some leaf shapes and color them the same colors as your butterfly. Make a branch using the cardboard and stick the leaves on top.
3. Now put the butterfly on top to see how it becomes camouflaged.

Moths often have similar colors and patterns as tree bark and dead leaf litter.

Shieldbugs have broad, flat bodies that look like the leaves around them.

Geometrid caterpillars have a brown, sticklike appearance.

Leafy wings
This butterfly looks just like a leaf. When it rests or feeds on a flower, it blends in with the plant.

AWESOME BUGS

Dinner time

Almost all insects eat plants. They feed on the sap (liquid) in stems and leaves, the nectar in flowers, and the soft flesh of fruits and berries. However, some insects prefer to eat their neighbors!

Stinky meal
Dung beetles roll animal droppings into big, round balls. They roll the balls into their nests and feed on them.

AWESOME BUGS

Nibbling wood
Termites feed on decaying wood, tree stumps, and the roots of plants.

Bee killer
The bee wolf is a large solitary wasp that preys on honeybees. It paralyzes them with its sting and carries them back to the nest to feed to its young.

FUN FACT!
Many insect species eat animal droppings. Some beetles lay their eggs in droppings, then the larvae hatch out and eat the dung!

Furniture beetles like to eat the dead parts of trees and wood.

Death's head hawk-moth caterpillars feed on potato plants and tomato leaves.

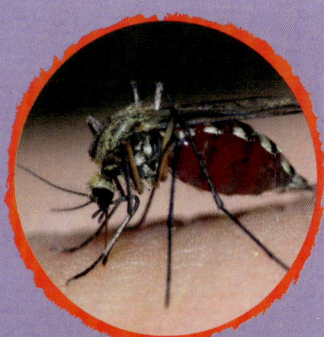

Mosquitoes feed on the blood of other animals, including humans.

AWESOME BUGS

What is a spider?

A spider is an arachnid. All spiders are expert hunters—they have fangs to grab and inject poison into prey. There are around 40,000 species of spiders in the world.

Spider anatomy
Spiders usually have eight eyes, eight legs, and are venomous. Their bodies are made up of two parts—the cephalothorax (head and thorax) and the abdomen (body).

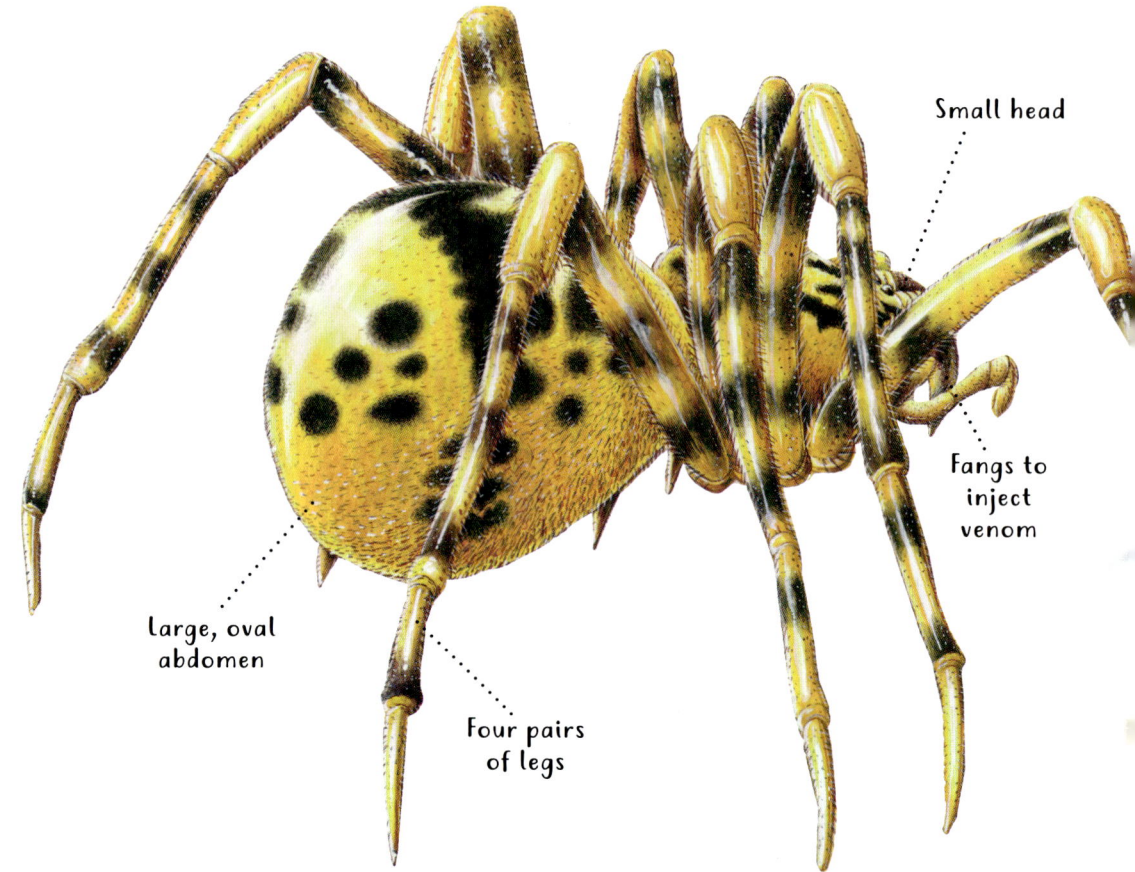

Small head

Fangs to inject venom

Large, oval abdomen

Four pairs of legs

AWESOME BUGS

Hundreds of babies
This crab spider is keeping watch over her web, in which hundreds of her spiderlings have hatched.

Tiny killer
The Australian redback spider belongs to the most deadly group of spiders—the widow spiders.

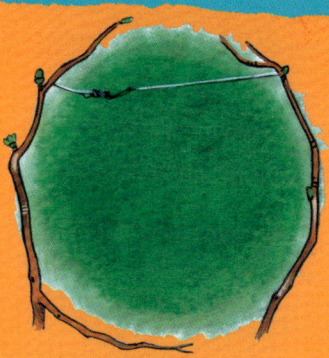

Stage 1
A spider starts a web by building a bridge.

Stage 2
More threads are added to make a strong framework.

Stage 3
The spider fills the frame with circular threads.

ANCIENT HISTORY

Life on the Nile

Without the river Nile, Egyptian civilization might never have existed. The Nile provided water for transport, drinking, and watering crops.

Papyrus reeds had many uses, including making boats and shoes.

Boats were the best way to get around in Egypt.

ANCIENT HISTORY

Blocks of stone for the pyramids were carried across the river.

Living on the Nile
Most Egyptians lived on the river's banks so they could grow crops. People spread further along the Nile as Egypt became more powerful.

Hunters caught hippos in the Nile.

Houses were built with mud from the river.

People spread further along the Nile as Egypt became more powerful.

ANCIENT HISTORY

Powerful pharaohs

The rulers of ancient Egypt were called pharaohs. Ordinary people believed that they were gods. The pharaoh was the most important and powerful person in the country.

Help to rule
Officials called viziers helped the pharaoh to rule Egypt. Each ruler chose two viziers. They were very powerful and important men.

ANCIENT HISTORY

Queen of Egypt

Hatshepsut was crowned pharaoh in 1473 BC when her husband, Thutmose II, died. She adopted the royal symbols of the double crown, the crook, the flail (whip)—and also the ceremonial beard!

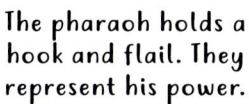

Ramses II ruled for more than 60 years. He was a great builder and a brave soldier.

The pharaoh holds a hook and flail. They represent his power.

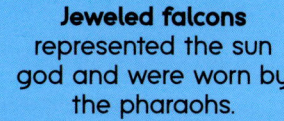

Jeweled falcons represented the sun god and were worn by the pharaohs.

FUN FACT!

Women courtiers sometimes wore hair cones made of animal fat. The melting fat trickled down their heads, making their hair smell sweet, but look greasy!

ANCIENT HISTORY

Gods and goddesses

The ancient Egyptians worshipped more than 1,000 different gods and goddesses. The most important was Ra, the sun god. A god was often shown as an animal, or half-human, half-animal.

Ra

King of the gods
At night, the sun god Ra traveled through the underworld and was born again each morning. According to the Egyptians, this was the reason the Sun rose each day.

FUN FACT!
Bastet was the goddess of cats, musicians, and dancers. Cats were sacred in ancient Egypt. When a pet cat died it was wrapped and buried in a cat-shaped coffin.

ANCIENT HISTORY

Anubis

Jackal-headed god
Anubis was in charge of preparing bodies to be mummified. As jackals were often found near cemeteries, Anubis was given the head of a jackal.

Osiris

The underworld
Osiris was the god of the dead. He and his wife Isis were in charge of the underworld. Ancient Egyptians believed that dead people traveled to the underworld.

Isis

Horus was the god of the sky. He had the head of a falcon.

Sobek was a god of the river Nile.

Tawaret represented mothers and young children.

ANCIENT HISTORY

The pyramids of Giza

The three pyramids at Giza are more than 4,500 years old. They were built for three kings—Khufu, Khafre, and Menkaure. After they died, their bodies were preserved as mummies and buried inside the pyramids.

The finished pyramids had a white coating to protect the stones underneath.

Blocks of stone were moved by wooden sleds.

The workers were given lots of water while working in the hot desert.

ANCIENT HISTORY

The biggest pyramid
The Great Pyramid is the biggest pyramid in the world. It was built with more than two million blocks.

FUN FACT!
A special guide for tomb robbers called "The Book of Buried Pearls" gave details of fabulous treasures hidden inside the pyramids!

The huge stones were levered into exactly the right position.

Teams of workers pulled the stones up the slopes.

The **Great Sphinx** at Giza has the body of a lion and the head of a human.

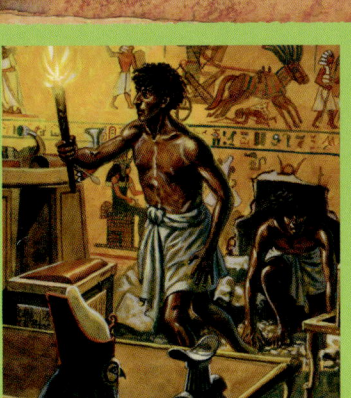

Breaking in
Tomb robbers broke into the pyramids to steal the treasures that were buried with the pharaohs.

The **Great Pyramid** had three smaller pyramids built next to it for King Khufu's wives.

ANCIENT HISTORY

Valley of the Kings

The ancient Egyptians built magnificent buildings, including temples and tombs. From 2150 BC, pharaohs were not buried in pyramids, but in tombs in the Valley of the Kings. Gods such as Ra were worshipped in temples.

The temple at Karnak
The courtyard at the temple of Amun Re at Karnak was entered through a massive gateway, or pylon, more than 55 feet tall.

ANCIENT HISTORY

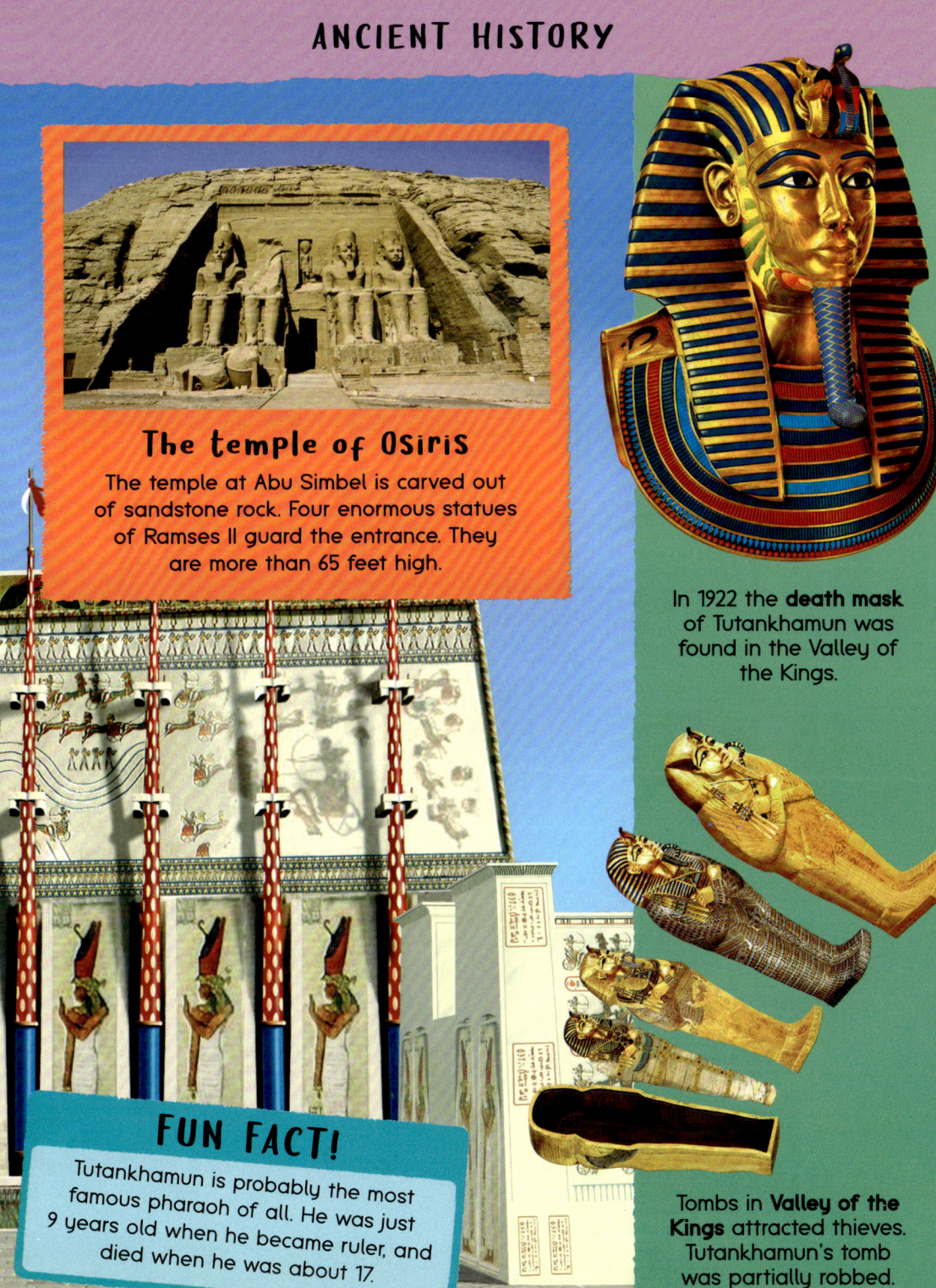

The temple of Osiris
The temple at Abu Simbel is carved out of sandstone rock. Four enormous statues of Ramses II guard the entrance. They are more than 65 feet high.

In 1922 the **death mask** of Tutankhamun was found in the Valley of the Kings.

FUN FACT!
Tutankhamun is probably the most famous pharaoh of all. He was just 9 years old when he became ruler, and died when he was about 17.

Tombs in **Valley of the Kings** attracted thieves. Tutankhamun's tomb was partially robbed.

ANCIENT HISTORY

Preserving the dead

Making a mummy was skilled work. The body's insides were removed, except for the heart. Next, the body was left to dry for 40 days. Then it was washed and filled with linen to keep its shape. Finally, the body was covered in oil and wrapped in linen bandages.

Hundreds of yards of bandages were used.

ANCIENT HISTORY

Priest wearing Anubis mask reads prayers.

Amulets (charms) placed inside bandages.

Wrapping the body in bandages took 11 days.

It took many years to become a **mummy-maker**.

The **mummy** was placed in a special case to be buried.

143

ANCIENT HISTORY

The Roman empire

Around 200 BC, Rome was the center of a great empire. It was rich and powerful, ruling more than 50 million people around the world. The Roman empire was made up of many different countries ruled by one person—the emperor.

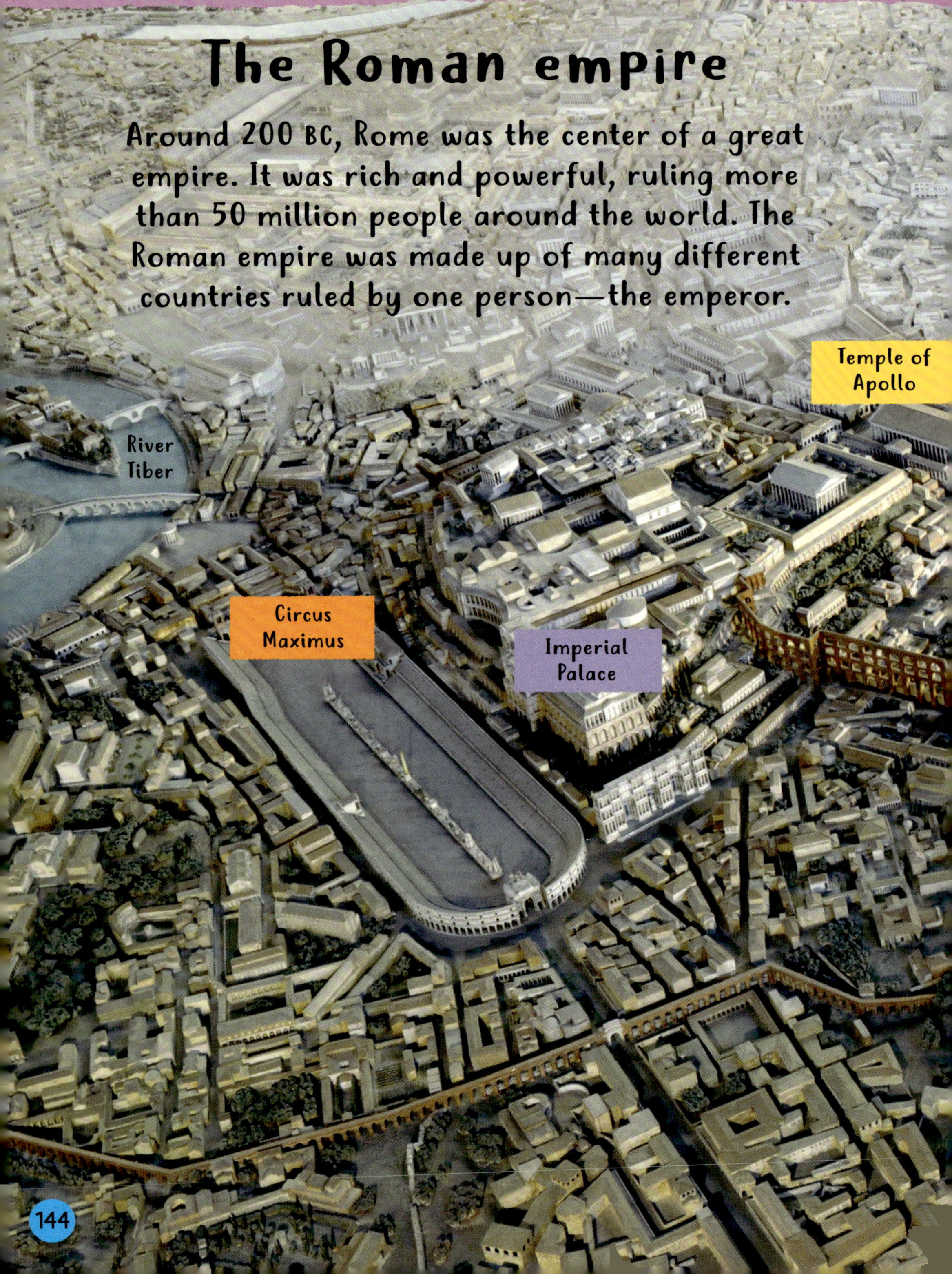

Temple of Apollo

River Tiber

Circus Maximus

Imperial Palace

ANCIENT HISTORY

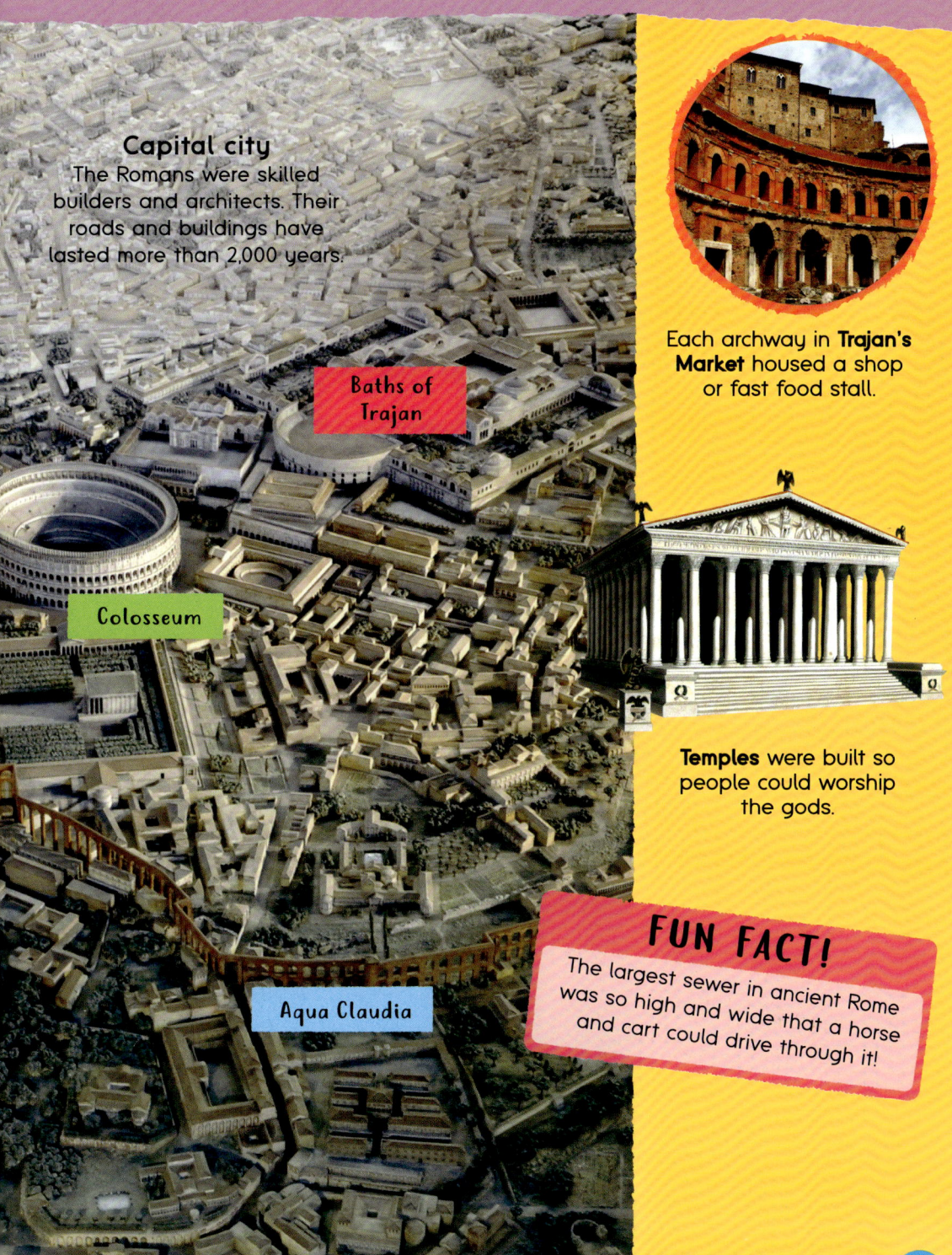

Capital city
The Romans were skilled builders and architects. Their roads and buildings have lasted more than 2,000 years.

Baths of Trajan

Colosseum

Aqua Claudia

Each archway in **Trajan's Market** housed a shop or fast food stall.

Temples were built so people could worship the gods.

FUN FACT!
The largest sewer in ancient Rome was so high and wide that a horse and cart could drive through it!

ANCIENT HISTORY

Family life

A Roman family included servants as well as a husband, wife, and their children. In rich families, the servants had their own quarters within the villas (homes).

Herbs were ground to put in sauces.

Cooking together
Families spent much of their time in the kitchen. Servants helped the women of the household to prepare the meals.

Wine and oil were stored in large pots.

ANCIENT HISTORY

Roman parties
At banquets, Romans ate lying down on couches around a main table. They took off their sandals before entering the dining room.

Grapes were crushed and made into wine.

The Romans ate a lot of fruits, and figs were very popular.

FUN FACT!
Only rich families had their own kitchens. Ordinary people went to *popinae* (cheap eating houses) or bought ready-cooked snacks from food stalls on streets.

Olives could be pickled and eaten with bread, or crushed to make oil.

ANCIENT HISTORY

A trip to the baths

Roman baths were places to wash, relax, meet friends, and get fit. Visitors could have a massage or a haircut. They could also buy scented oils and perfumes, read a book, eat, or admire works of art.

The Great Bath was adorned with statues.

Luxury baths
One of the most popular baths was at Aquae Sulis (Bath, England). It had changing rooms and lockers, as well as hot, warm, and cold baths.

Hot springs
The Romans believed that the heat of the water used at Aquae Sulis was the mystical work of the gods. Now we know that the water source was an ancient hot spring.

Today only the actual water bath at Aquae Sulis is original, the other buildings date from the 18th century.

ANCIENT HISTORY

Underfloor heating

Baths were centrally heated! Blasts of hot air warmed by a wood-burning furnace circulated in channels built beneath the floor.

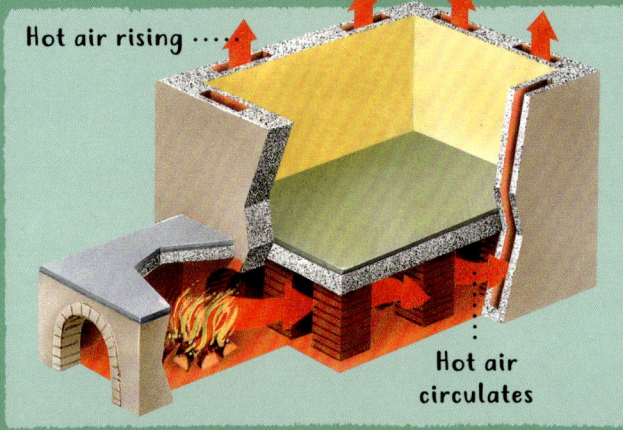

Hot air rising

Hot air circulates

The Baths of Caracalla included libraries, shops, and gardens.

Romans often played **board games** at the baths.

FUN FACT!

Men and women did not bathe together. Women usually went to the baths in the morning, and men went in the afternoon.

ANCIENT HISTORY

Roman style

What a Roman wore depended on how important they were. Ordinary people wore plain white togas made of rough material. The rich wore robes made of fine-quality wool and silk.

Looking good
At the height of the empire, women wore brightly colored robes and shawls.

Servants helped with hair and makeup.

Purple was the most expensive dye in ancient Rome.

Both men and women wore makeup.

ANCIENT HISTORY

Wear a Roman toga

1 Drape a white sheet over your left shoulder. Then pass the rest behind your back.

2 Pull the sheet across your front, so that you're wrapped up in it.

3 Finally, drape the last end over your right hand and there you have it, a Roman toga!

A Roman **comb** was made of ivory, bone, or wood.

FUN FACT!
The Romans liked to smell sweet. Perfume was made with flowers from southern Europe, spices from India, and sweet-smelling resin from Arabia.

Gems and jewels
Roman women wore fine jewelry made of gold and pearls. A shiny black stone called jet was carved into bangles and beads.

Necklace set with jewels

Gold earrings

Jet bangle

Gold ring

Hairstyles took a long time to fix and were kept in place with pins.

ANCIENT HISTORY

The mighty Colosseum

A huge oval arena in the center of Rome, the Colosseum could seat 50,000 people. It was built of stone, concrete, and marble and had 80 separate entrances. The grand opening in AD 80 was the first gladiator games, which lasted 100 days.

Colosseum today

Even in 21st century Rome, the Colosseum is remarkably well preserved. It is visited by millions of tourists each year.

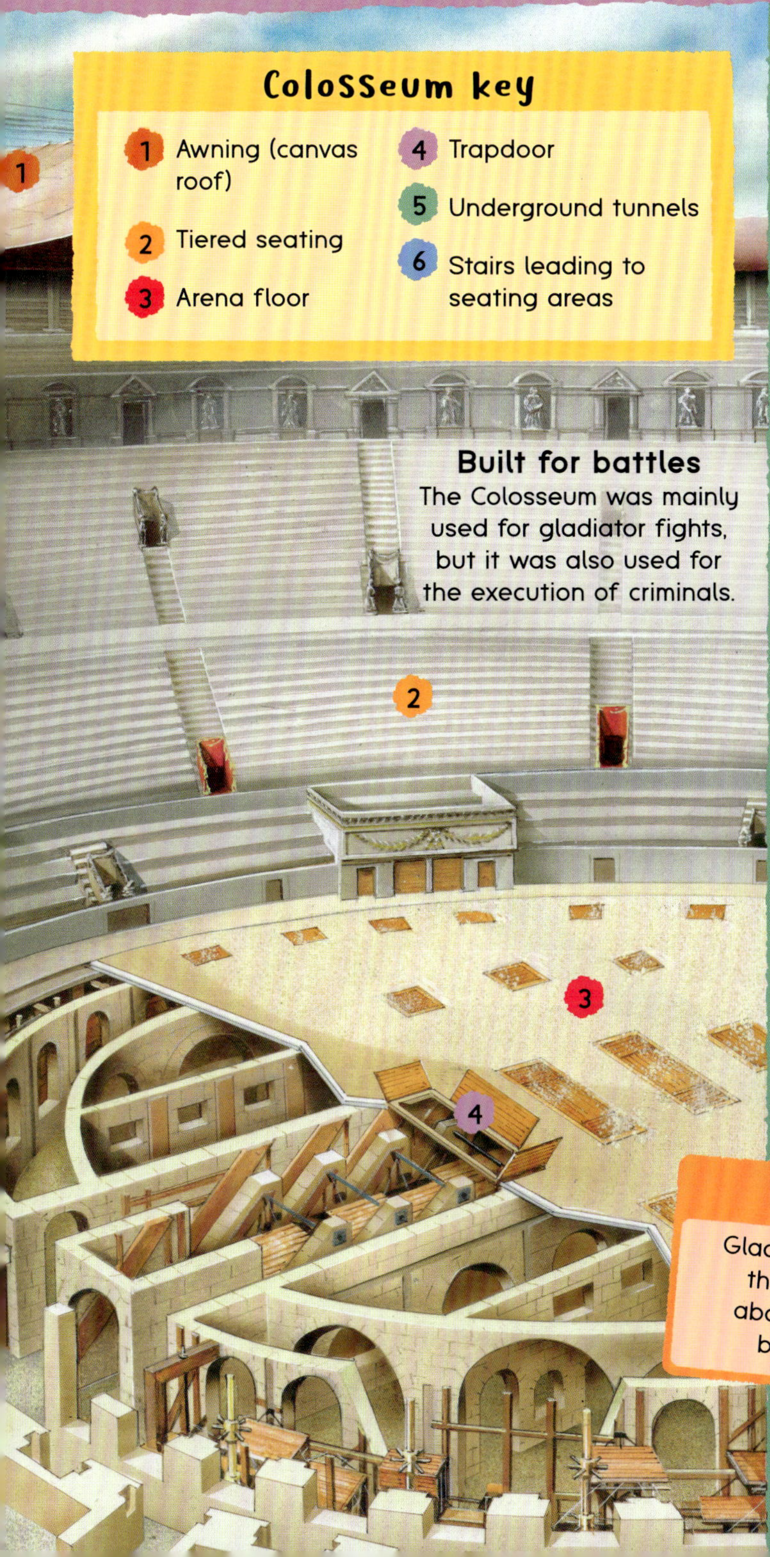

ANCIENT HISTORY

Colosseum key

1. Awning (canvas roof)
2. Tiered seating
3. Arena floor
4. Trapdoor
5. Underground tunnels
6. Stairs leading to seating areas

Built for battles
The Colosseum was mainly used for gladiator fights, but it was also used for the execution of criminals.

Gladiator **helmets** were decorated with plumes and crests to make them look taller or bigger.

Gladiators were named after a short, stabbing sword called the **gladius**.

FUN FACT!
Gladiators became so popular that people wrote graffiti about them on the walls of buildings around Rome.

ANCIENT HISTORY

In the army

The Roman empire needed troops to defend its land against enemy attack. It was a dangerous job, but the soldiers were well paid and cared for. After around 25 years of service, they were given money or land.

FUN FACT!
Roman soldiers kept warm in cold countries by wearing wooly underwear beneath their tunics!

On the move
The Roman army marched around the empire to where they were needed. They traveled up to 20 miles a day!

ANCIENT HISTORY

Tortoise Shell

During battles, soldiers used their shields to make a protective "shell" called a testudo, or tortoise. Their shields were placed at all sides.

Roman cavalry soldiers rode horses and helped the foot soldiers during battle.

Roman armor was made from metal strips held together by straps and buckles.

The **ballista** was a weapon that could hurl a heavy javelin over a range of 550 yards.

INDEX

A
Age of Dinosaurs 70
agoutis 99
airplanes 45
algae 33
Allosaurus 75
Amazon rain forest 41
Antarctica 38, 94
antelopes 115
ants 120
Anubis 137
Apatosaurus 73
apes 98
Apollo butterflies 123
Aquae Sulis (Bath) 148
Arabian Desert 39
Arabian Sea 43
arachnids 118, 119, 130–131
Arctic 94
Arctic hares 94
Arctic Ocean 42
Arctic terns 111
Argentinosaurus 73
Ariane 5 24, 25
armor 155
astronauts 15, 26, 27
Atacama Desert 39
Atlantic Ocean 42
atmosphere 11, 13, 17, 29, 44–45
atom bombs 58
atoms 62, 66–67
aye-ayes 99

B
bald eagles 106, 117
baleen 97
bamboo 88
banquets 147
barn owls 113
Barosaurus 72
baths, Roman 148–149
bats 86, 98
batteries 63
battles 154
beaks 114–115
bears 90, 94
beavers 83
bee-eaters 114
bees 120, 125
beetles 121, 123, 125, 128, 129
Bering Sea 42
bird cake 109

birds 102–117
birds of prey 116–117
bites 124–125
block mountains 31
blood-suckers 118
blue whales 86–87
bombardier beetles 125
booster engines 24
box guitar 59
Brachiosaurus 73
brain 59
breathing equipment 44
bridges 65
brimstone butterflies 127
brown bears 90
bugs 118–131
building materials 53
butterflies 120, 123, 127

C
cables 62
camels 39, 101
cameras 57
camouflage 95, 126–127
candles 54, 55
canopic jars 142
capybaras 87
carbon dioxide 16
carbon fiber 64
Caribbean Sea 42
carnivores 71, 74–75, 80, 90–91
caterpillars 127, 129
cavalry 155
cave swiftlets 107
caves 36–37
centipedes 119
cephalothorax 130
ceramics 65
Ceres 19
chambers 36–37
charcoal 147
chariots 144
Charon 19
chicks 102, 103, 105
chimps 85
cirrus clouds 51
Citipati 76
civets 98
climates 46–47
clothing, Roman 150–151, 155
clouds 17, 22, 23, 50, 51
cockchafer beetles 121

collective nouns, mammals 85
colonies 85
Colosseum 152–153
colors 57
combs 151
compound eyes 123
concrete 53
conduction 55
coniferous forests 40, 41
convection 55
core, Earth's 28, 29
corona 9
cotton 65
crab spider 131
craters 14, 15, 18, 19, 23
crescent Moon 15
Cretaceous Period 71
crust, Earth's 28, 29, 30, 31
crystals 37
cumulonimbus clouds 51

D
day and night 49
death masks 141, 142
death's head hawk-moth caterpillars 129
decibels 58
deciduous forests 40
deer 87
Deinonychus 71
deltas 32
desert animals 101–101
desert roses 39
deserts 38–39, 46, 47, 100–101
dinosaurs 70–81
Diplodocus 73
dogs 90
dolphins 82, 96–97
dragonflies 123
drizzle 51
duck-billed platypuses 93
ducks 108, 109, 111
dung beetles 128
dusky dolphins 82
dwarf planets 18, 19
dyes 150

E
eagles 106, 111, 116–117
ears 59
Earth 9, 10, 11, 12–13, 14, 28–35, 48–49

Earth's layers 28–29
earwigs 121
echoes 59
eclipses 9
egg tooth 104
eggs (birds) 102, 104–105, 114
eggs (dinosaurs) 76, 77, 78, 79, 81
Egypt, ancient 132–143
Egyptian vultures 114
eider ducks 108
electric circuits 63
electricity 27, 53, 60, 62–63
electromagnets 60, 61
electrons 62, 66, 67
elephants 86
elytra 122
embryos 77
emperor penguins 103, 104
emperors 144
empires 144
emus 105
energy 53, 54, 56, 62
Equator 46
Eris 19
European bee-eaters 114
evening star 17
exosphere 45
eyes 113, 123

F
falcons 108, 135, 137
fall 40, 49
family life, Roman 146–147
fangs 130
fennec foxes 101
filter-feeding 97
fireworks 54
flash floods 50
flies 120, 121
flippers 96, 97
floods 50, 133
fold mountains 30
food, Roman 147
foot soldiers 155
footwear, Roman 151
forces 52, 61
forests 40–41, 46, 49
fossils 69, 70, 76, 78, 80
furniture beetles 129

G
galaxies 13
Galilean moons 21
Galileo Galilei 21

games, Roman 152–153
gannets 111
gas giants 22
gases 8, 13, 16, 54, 67
geese 105, 108
gems 151
generators 63
gentoo penguins 111
geometrid caterpillars 127
gerbils 101
giant pandas 88
gibbous Moon 15
Gibson Desert 39
Giganotosaurus 75
giraffes 87, 89
Giza 138–139
glaciers 34–35
gladiators 152, 153
glass 65
Gobi Desert 39, 101
gods and goddesses,
   Egyptian 133, 134, 136–137, 140
golden eagles 116
Gorgosaurus 68
goslings 105
graffiti 153
granite 29
grasslands 47
gravity 10, 24, 52
gray whales 97
Great Basin Desert 39
Great Hall at Karnak 140
Great Pyramid 139
Great Red Spot 20
Great Sandy Desert 39
Great Sphinx 139
Great Victoria Desert 39
Guanlong 69
guillemots 103

H
hair cones 135
hairstyles, Egyptian 135
hairstyles, Roman 151
half Moon 15
hares 94, 95
harp seals 95
Hatshepsut 135
hawks 116, 117
heat 54–55
helium 67
helmets 153
herbivores 71, 80, 88–89, 128–129

herbs 146
herds 84
Himalayas 31
hippos 92, 93, 133
hives 120–121
hog-nosed bats 86
honeybees 120–121
hornets 125
horses 155
Horus 137
hummingbirds 109, 115
humpback whales 97
hydrogen 67
hydrothermal vents 43
hyenas 101

I
ice caps 16
icebergs 43, 34, 35
incubation 103, 105
Indian Ocean 42, 43
insects 118, 120–129
International Space Station (ISS) 26–27
Io 21
Isis 137

J
jackals 137, 143
jaguars 98
jet 151
jet engines 58
jewelry 135, 151
Jupiter 10, 11, 20, 21
Jurassic Period 71

K
kangaroo rats 101
killer whales 97
kitchens 146–147
kiwis 113
koalas 85
Kuwait 43

L
ladybugs 120, 121, 122
lakes 33
larvae 125
lava 30
leaf insects 126
lemurs 89, 99
light 56–57
light rays 56
light, speed of 57
light waves 56, 57

limestone 37, 65
lions 85, 90
lizards 47
loudspeakers 59

M

Maat Mons 17
maglev (magnetic levitation) trains 61
magnetic field 61
magnets and magnetism 60–61
Maiasaura 78–79
mallards 109
mammals 71, 82–91
manatees 93
mantle, Earth's 28
market places 145
Mars 10, 11, 16
masks 141, 142
materials 64–65
meanders 33
Mediterranean Sea 42, 43
meerkats 85
meltwater 35
Mercury 10, 11, 18, 19
mesosphere 45
Mesozoic Era 70
meteorites 45, 80
milk, mother's 83
millipedes 119
minerals 33, 36, 37, 39, 43
mirrors 57
mites 119
Mojave Desert 39
mollusks 119
molten rock 29
monkeys 98
Moon 9, 10, 11, 14–15
Moon, phases of the 15
moons 17, 18, 19, 21, 23
mosquitoes 123
moths 127, 129
Mount Everest 31
mountain peaks 31
mountaineers 31, 44
mountains 30–31, 46, 47
mouse deer 87
mummies 137, 138, 142–143
mushroom stones 35
musk oxen 95
myriapods 119

N

natron 143

nebulae 13
nectar 115, 120
Neptune 10, 22, 23
nests (birds) 105, 106–107
nests (dinosaurs) 78–79
neutrons 66, 67
Nile, river 132–133, 137
North and South poles 47, 48, 49
northern gannets 111
Northern Hemisphere 48, 49
nucleus 66
nuthatches 115

O

oases 39
Oberon 23
oceans 42–43
oil 65, 146, 147
olives 147
Olympus Mons 16
opossums 92
orangutans 83
orbit 25
Osiris 137, 141
ostriches 103
otters 92
Oviraptor 76
owls 105, 112–113, 116
oxbow lakes 33
oxpeckers 115
oxygen 44, 67

P

Pacific Ocean 42, 43
pandas 83, 88
pangolins 83
papyrus 132
payload 25
penguins 103, 104, 105, 110, 111
peregrine falcons 108
Persian Gulf 43
pharaohs 134–135, 139
Philippine eagles 116
Phobos 17
planetary rings 11, 21, 22, 23
planets 10–11, 18–23
plastics 65
plates, Earth's 29
Pluto 10, 18
poison 124, 130
polar bears 94
polar climates 47
polar deserts 38
poles, magnetic 61

poles, North and South 47, 48, 49
pollen 120
poorwills 113
pottos 98
power plants 62, 63
praying mantises 124
prides 85
prisms 56
protons 66, 67
puffins 115
pushes and pulls 52
pygmy shrews 87
pyramids 132, 138–139

R

Ra 136, 140
rabbits 89
racing cars 64
rain 50, 51
rain forest animals 98–99
rain forests 40, 73, 47, 98–99
rain gauge 51
rainbows 56
rainwater, acidic 37
Ramses II 135
rats 92, 101
red pandas 83
redback spiders 131
redwoods 41
reflection 57
refraction 57
reptiles 68
rhinos 89
ring-tailed lemurs 99
river birds 16
river mammals 92–93
rivers 32–33, 51
rockets 24–25
rodents 87, 117
rollercoasters 52
Roman empire 144, 154
Rome, ancient 144–155
Rome, city of 144–317, 152–153

S

Sahara Desert 39
sand dunes 39
Sarawak Chamber 37
satellites 45
Saturn 10, 20, 21
sauropods 71, 72–73
schools of dolphins 96
science 52–67
scorpionflies 121

sea lions 96
sea stacks 43
seals 87, 95, 96
seas 14, 42
seasons 48–49
secretary birds 116
senses 112
servants 146
shieldbugs 127
shields 155
shoes 151
shrews 87
silk 150
Simpson Desert 39
skiing 49
Skylab 27
skyscrapers 53
sloths 99
snails 119
snakes 116
snow leopards 95
snowboarding 49
snowshoe hares 95
Sobek 137
solar eclipses 9
solar flares 8
solar panels 27, 63
solar prominences 8, 9
Solar System 10–11, 13, 20, 21
soldiers 154–155
sound waves 58, 59
sounds 58–59
South China Sea 43
Southern Ocean 43
Soyuz spacecraft 27
space 8–27
space exploration 24–27, 53
space stations 26–27
spacecraft 25, 26–27
spectrum 56
spiders 119
Spinosaurus 75
spring 40, 48
springs 32
squirrels 41
stalagmites and stalactites 36, 37
stars 13, 17
steel 53, 61
stick insects 126
stings 121, 124–125
stoop 108
storms 16, 20, 22
stratosphere 45
stratus clouds 51

streams 32, 33
subatomic particles 66
summer 48, 49
Sun 8–9, 10, 19, 48, 49
sun god 136
sunspots 8, 9
swallows 107, 109
swans 105
swords 153

T

talons 116
tapirs 99
Tawaret 137
telescopes 15
temperate climate 46
temperate forests 40, 41
temperate grassland 47
temples 133, 140–141, 145
termites 129
thermometers 55
thermosphere 45
thorax 122, 130
thunderstorms 58
ticks 115, 118, 119
tigers 90, 91
togas 151
tomb robbers 139, 141
total eclipses 9
toucans 41
transmission towers 62, 63
transport 53
Triassic Period 70
tropical forest 46
tropical grassland 47
troposphere 45
tunics 150
tusks 95
Tutankhamun 141
tyrannosaurs 68, 69, 74–75
Tyrannosaurus rex 69, 74–75, 77

U, V

underworld 136, 137
Uranus 10, 22, 23
Valles Marineris 17
Valley of the Kings 140–141
valleys 35
Venus 10, 11, 16, 17
viziers 134
volcanic mountains 30
volcanoes 16, 17, 21, 29, 81
voles 92
vultures 114, 115

W

walruses 95
warm-blooded animals 82
wars 144
washing 149
wasps 124, 125
water cycle 50–51
water opossum 92
water rats 92
water vapor 50, 51
water voles 92
waterfalls 33, 37
wax 54, 121
weapons 153
weather 84–51
weaver birds 107
webs 131
whales 86–87, 96, 97
white light 56
widow spiders 131
wildebeest 101
wine 146
wings 109, 122, 123
winter 49
wolves 85, 90, 91
wombats 89
wood 65
woodpeckers 105
worms 119

Y, Z

years 16
zebras 84–85

ACKNOWLEDGMENTS

All artworks are from the Miles Kelly Artwork Bank

The publishers would like to thank the following sources for the use of their photographs:
(t = top, b = bottom, l = left, r = right, c = center, bg = background)

Dreamstime 37(cr) Paul Hakimata; 56(bg) Theo Gottwald

European Space Agency 17(cr) ESA/DLR/FU Berlin (G.Neukum)

Fotolia 33(tl) .shock, (cr) John Saxenian; 35(br) Alexander Zotov; 41(tr) Urbanhearts; 83(cr) rkwphotography; 85(cl) Helen Filatova; 101(tr) Vibe Images; 115(cr) javarman

iStock 15(phases of the moon) Castleski; 21(cr) ppart; 26-27(bc) Jan Rysavy; 39(cr) naes, (br) pkruger; 65(cr) Willette Photography, Inc

Nasa 9(bc) The Exploratorium, (cr) SDO/Solar Dynamics Observatory; 13(tr) X-ray: NASA/CXC; UV: NASA/JPL-Caltech; Optical: NASA/ESA/STScI/AURA; IR: NASA/JPL-Caltech/Univ. of Ariz, (br) ESA; 15(br); 17(br); 23(bl) JPL; 25(br) JPL/KSC; 27(br)

ShutterstockPremier 9(tc) Triff; 13(tc) arcelClemens; 29(tr) XYZ, (cr) beboy, (br) Alex Staroseltsev; 31(tc) Alexandr Zyryanov, (tr) Andrey_Popov, (cr) Jakub Cejpek; 32(bl) Mogens Trolle; 33 (cl meander) & (bl oxbow lake) Qba from Poland, (br) Pixmax; 34(bl) Michael Klenetsky; 35 (tr) mountainpix, (cr) Lee Price; 36(bl) Joshua Haviv; 37(br) Filip Fuxa; 38(cl) Armin Rose; 38-39(bg) rjmiguel; 39(tr) Patrick Poendl; 40-41(bg) Antonio Jorge Nunes; 41(tc) buteo, (bc) Jacob Whyman, (cr) USBFCO, (br) Rena Schild; 42(cl) IM_photo, (cr) Valery Bareta; 43(cl) Nasser Buhamad, (cr) Christopher Meder, (br) Volodymyr Goinyk; 44(bg) Mikadun, (cr) MarcelClemens; 45(tr) Paul Fleet, (cr) Triff, (br) IM_photo; 46 (tl desert icon) apstockphoto, (cl mountain icon) Fat Jackey, (bl tropical forest) szefei; 47 (c, icon 1) Oleg Znamenskiy, (c, icon 2) John De Bord, (c, icon 3) kkaplin, (c, icon 4) Richard Semik, (c, icon 5) sima, (c, icon 6) Sergey Toronto, (tr) haveseen, (cr) Fat Jackey, (br) Brian Lasenby; 48(bc) artjazz, (cr) Mark Bridger; 49 (c icon) Michael Macsuga, (bl) S.Borisov, (tr) Jan kranendonk, (br) IM_photo; 50(cl) Kamonrat; 51(tr) Serg64, (cr) elen_studio, (br) Sergey Sergeev; 52-53(bg) Jabiru; 53(tc) Songquan Deng, (tr) Ibooo7, (cr) Pablo Scapinachis; 54(bl) joingate; 54-55(bg) DeymosHR; 55(tr) Litvinenko Anastasia, (cr) Ivonne Wierink, (br) Serhiy Shullye; 57(bl) bioraven, (bc) robodread, (br) Chiyacat; 58(cl) Pablo Scapinachis, (bl) Jennifer Griner, 59(cr) Peter Gudella, (br) SergiyN; 60(bg) Vadim Kozlovsky; 61(bl) YegoroV, (tr) revers, (cr) arosoft; 62(b) Ray Hub; 63(tr) Smileus, (cr) dslaven, (br) Kodda; 64(bg) Jaggat Rashidi; 65(bl) Mike Flippo, (tr) Wim Claes, (br) Christian Mueller; 66-67(bg) Mrjafari; 73(tl) Catmando, (cl) Michael Rosskothen, (bl) Catmando; 75(tr) Linda Bucklin, (cr) Kostiantyn Ivanyshen; 81(br) Mana Photo; 83(br) Eric Gevaert, (br) Tathoms; 84(b) TravelMediaProductions; 85(tl) Meawpong3405, (tc) Wolfgang Kruck, (c, prairie dogs) Henk Bentlage, (tr) Riaan van den Berg, (cr) Andras Deak, (br) anetapics; 86(bc) Michael Wick; 87(bc) Christian Musat, (tr) sunsetman, (cr) Christian Musat, (br) Rudmer Zwerver; 89(tc) Henk Paul, (tr) kyslynskahal, (cr) Ronsmith, (br) Robyn Butler, (bl) hakoar; 90(bg) Manamana; 91(tc) Peter Betts, (tr) Ron Hilton, (cr) Debbie Aird Designs, (br) Sergey Uryadnikov; 92(bl) Cat Downie; 93(tr) Liquid Productions, LLC, (cr) alanf; 94(bg) Anette Holmberg, 95(tl) Dennis W Donohue, (bl) & (tr) Vladimir Melnik, (cr) Samsem, (br) Nialat; 96(bg) Blaine Image, (bc) Mariusz Potocki; 97(tc) Marcelo Sanchez, (tr) Jo Crebbin, (cr) Four Oaks, (br) Xavier MARCHANT; 98(bc) ANDRE DIB; 99(tr) Ammit Jack; 100(bg) HainaultPhoto; 101(tl) Hedrus, (cr) EcoPrint; 102(cl) Steve Byland, (bc) wizdata; 103(bl) Sue McDonald, (tr) Marcin Sylwia Ciesielski, (cr) John Carnemolla, (br) David Evison; 104(cr) Mary Beth Charles; 105(tl) Ewan Chesser, (bc) Eric Isselee, (tr) aaltair, (cr) TravelMediaProductions; 106(bg) Kane513; 107(tc) Johan Swanepoel, (tr) FloridaStock, (cr) A_SH, (br) Fredy Thuerig; 108(bg) MCarter; 109(bg) Natalia Sinjushina & Evgeniy Meyke, (tr) Steve Byland, (cr) Tomatito, (br) Stubblefield Photography; 110(bg) Rich Lindie; 111(tl) Arto Hakola, (bl) Daniel-Alvarez, (tr) Marek CECH, (cr) Milan M Ju, (br) Mark Medcalf; 113(br) Eric Isselee; 114(tl) aabeele; 115(tc) Karel Gallas, (bl) Joe Gough, (tr) Sari ONeal, (br) Villiers Steyn; 117(tr) ArvydasS, (cr) BearFotos, (br) Justin Black; 118(br) Tobik; 119(trl) GraphicsRF, (bl) Dusty Cline, (tr) TTstudio, (br) Audrey Snider-Bell; 120(bl) Cathy Keifer; 121(tr) Karel Gallas, (cr) Kletr, (br) Volkov Alexey; 123(bl) alslutsky, (tr) jps, (br) Jan-Nor Photography; 124(b) Cathy Keifer; 125(tl) vblinov, (tr) Matt Jeppson, (cr) Ryan M. Bolton, (br) Biehler Michael; 126(bl) Johan Larson, (br) kurt_G; 127(bc) Fabien Monteil, (tr) Wilm Ihlenfeld, (cr) olavs, (br) Tyler Fox; 128(bg) Nick Stubbs; 129(tc) Dr Morley Read, (bc) Milkovasa, (br) Pasi Koskela; 131(tc) Dariusz Majgier; 135(tr) ChameleonsEye; 141(tl) WitR, 144-145(bg) Croato; 145(tr) airy; 147(tr) Dionisvera, (br) Yulia Davidovich, (br) Valentyn Volkov; 149(tr) Viacheslav Lopatin; 152(cl) ESB Professional

Every effort has been made to acknowledge the source and copyright holder of each picture. Miles Kelly Publishing apologizes for any unintentional errors or omissions.